1971

AGRARIAN AGE

A Background for Wordsworth

BY

KENNETH MacLEAN

ARCHON BOOKS
1970

[*Yale Studies in English, Vol. 115*]

SBN: 208 00925 6
Library of Congress Catalog Card Number: 70-91185
Printed in the United States of America

FOR

PAUL, DAVID, AND BURTON

PREFATORY NOTE

IN THESE essays, tentative and experimental as they are, that strong agrarian sentiment controlling the development of literature and art in the later eighteenth century has been put side by side with certain aspects of the economic life and thought of that time. Seen thus against the currents of the agricultural revolution and within the patterns of agrarian economic theory, the social relevance of the literature of the "agrarian age" becomes somewhat more evident. How slightly the essential social meaning of romantic literature has (until just recently) been considered, those know best who are familiar with the criticism bearing upon this period. To be sure, the search for social reference in literature will ignore inevitably its best meaning and importance. But such studies may be carried through with the persuasion that it is the best values of literature which give importance to its simple moral intentions.

To describe the later eighteenth century as an agrarian age is in a sense to ignore its most important economic feature, namely, the beginnings of industrialism. Obviously it is not my intention to overlook this primary social fact. Yet there was enough agrarian feeling in this period—partly rising in opposition to industrialism, but partly arising more independently and more deeply from cultural traditions—to make this description by no means ironical.

The reading for this study was done some time ago. I regret that the notes do not include references to such recent books as Jacob Bronowski's *William Blake, 1757–1827; a Man without a Mask* (London, Secker & Warburg, 1944), T. S. Ashton's *The Industrial Revolution, 1760–1830* (Home University Library. London, Oxford University Press, 1948), and A. Whitney Griswold's *Farming and Democracy* (New York, Harcourt, Brace, 1948). I regret too that I did not use an earlier study of great value in writing these essays, Naomi Riches' *The Agricultural Revolution in Norfolk* (Chapel Hill, University of North Carolina Press, 1937). The bibliography relevant to this subject is growing. Recent volumes of *Agricultural History* include such articles as Carl B. Cone's "Edmund Burke, the Farmer" (xix [1945], 65–69), and E. A. Parker's and R. M. Williams', "John Dyer, the Poet, as Farmer" (xxii [1948], 134–41).

The illustrations are woodcuts by Thomas Bewick (1753–1828). The plates for these reproductions have been made from original Bewick blocks through the kindness of T. Hunter Middleton of Chicago, who founded the Cherryburn Press in Bewick's honor and printed in

1945 the *Thomas Bewick Portfolio,* using a selection of the original blocks in his own collection. Eleven of the thirteen illustrations here used are from Mr. Middleton's collection. Two plates, those for pages 58 and 86, have been made from Bewick blocks in the Newberry Library, Chicago, and they are reproduced by the kind permission of Stanley Pargellis, the Librarian.

I have many friends to thank now that these essays are appearing in the Yale Studies in English, and first, Benjamin Nangle, the editor. A most generous grant for this book has been made by the Department of English of the University of Toronto, and I greatly appreciate this kindness on the part of my colleagues. Elizabeth McMullan of the Yale University Press has given me excellent editorial assistance. Esther Davison and Conway Turton were most helpful in preparing the manuscript. In carrying through these studies I received the most friendly advice from Lewis Curtis. John Robins and Wallace Notestein also gave me help and criticism for which I am grateful. Finally, I have to express my obligation to Chauncey Tinker. To him and to the Yale University Library, which is now so much his care, I am indeed indebted.

KENNETH MACLEAN

Victoria College,
University of Toronto.

CONTENTS

CUE TITLES

Annals   *Annals of Agriculture.* Arthur Young, ed. London and Bury St. Edmund's, 1784–1815. 46 vols.

Clapham   J. H. Clapham. *An Economic History of Modern Britain.* Cambridge, Cambridge University Press, 1926–38. 3 vols.

Curtler   W. H. R. Curtler. *Short History of English Agriculture.* Oxford, Clarendon Press, 1909.

Dict. Pol. Econ.   *Dictionary of Political Economy.* R. H. Inglis Palgrave, ed. London, Macmillan, 1894–99. 3 vols.

DNB   *Dictionary of National Biography.*

Early Letters   *Early Letters of William and Dorothy Wordsworth.* Ernest de Selincourt, ed. Oxford, Clarendon Press, 1935.

Gent. Mag.   *Gentleman's Magazine.*

Gide and Rist   Charles Gide and Charles Rist. *History of Economic Doctrines.* R. Richards, tr. London, George G. Harrap, 1937.

Gilpin, *Observations*   William Gilpin. *Observations, Relative Chiefly to Picturesque Beauty, Made in the Year 1772, on Several Parts of England; Particularly the Mountains, and Lakes of Cumberland, and Westmoreland.* 2d ed. London, 1788. 2 vols.

Gonner   E. C. K. Gonner. *Common Land and Inclosure.* London, Macmillan, 1912.

Gray   H. L. Gray. *English Field Systems.* Cambridge, Mass., Harvard University Press, 1915.

Hamilton   Henry Hamilton. *The Industrial Revolution in Scotland.* Oxford, Clarendon Press, 1932.

Hammond   John L. Hammond and Barbara Ham-
                           mond. *The Village Labourer, 1760–
                           1832.* 4th ed. London, Longmans,
                           Green, 1936.
Harper   G. M. Harper. *William Wordsworth.*
                           3d ed. London, John Murray, 1929.
Johnson   A. H. Johnson. *Disappearance of the
                           Small Landowner.* Oxford, Clarendon
                           Press, 1909.
Journals   *Journals of Dorothy Wordsworth.* Er-
                           nest de Selincourt, ed. London, Macmil-
                           lan, 1941. 2 vols.
Lecky   W. E. H. Lecky. *History of England
                           in the Eighteenth Century.* New York,
                           D. Appleton, 1878–90. 8 vols.
Lectures . . . Glasgow   Adam Smith. *Lectures on Justice, Po-
                           lice, Revenue and Arms, Delivered in
                           the University of Glasgow . . . Re-
                           ported by a Student in 1763.* E. Cannan,
                           ed. Oxford, Clarendon Press, 1896.
Letters . . . Middle Years *Letters of William and Dorothy Words-
                           worth: the Middle Years.* Ernest de
                           Selincourt, ed. Oxford, Clarendon Press,
                           1937. 2 vols.
Mantoux   Paul Mantoux. *The Industrial Revolu-
                           tion in the Eighteenth Century.* M. Ver-
                           non, tr. Rev. ed. New York, Harcourt,
                           Brace, 1935.
Memoir   *A Memoir of Thomas Bewick, Written
                           by Himself.* Newcastle-on-Tyne, 1862.
Prose Works   *The Prose Works of William Words-
                           worth.* A. B. Grosart, ed. London, Ed-
                           ward Moxon, Son, 1876. 3 vols.
Rural Rides   William Cobbett. *Rural Rides.* Every-
                           man ed. London, J. M. Dent & Sons.
                           n.d. 2 vols.
Toynbee   Arnold Toynbee. *Lectures on the In-
                           dustrial Revolution in England.* Lon-
                           don, Rivingtons, 1884.

Wealth of Nations	Adam Smith. *An Inquiry into the Nature and Causes of the Wealth of Nations.* J. E. Thorold Rogers, ed. Oxford, Clarendon Press, 1869. 2 vols.
Weulersse	Georges Weulersse. *Le Mouvement physiocratique en France (de 1756 à 1770).* Paris, Felix Alcan, 1910. 2 vols.
Wordsworth, *Poetical Works*	*The Poetical Works of Wordsworth.* Thomas Hutchinson, ed. Rev. ed., Ernest de Selincourt. London, Oxford University Press, 1936.

AGRARIAN AGE: A BACKGROUND FOR WORDSWORTH

I

The Agricultural Revolution: Poets, Peasants, and the Land

1. Agricultural Improvement in England

ENGLISH agriculture was revolutionized in the eighteenth century by a series of remarkable improvements which, whether they represented ideas imported from the Low Countries or developed at home, were an expression of the growing scientific spirit in England. Experiments heralding change were sufficiently conspicuous in 1726 to be satirized in the reactionary pages of *Gulliver's Travels*, where we read that the Grand Academy of Lagado had developed a brilliant new way of plowing, namely, by planting acorns in fields for swine to rout.[1] Foremost among the new scientists of agriculture was Jethro Tull, of Prosperous Farm on the borders of Berkshire. To Tull's farm at Shalborne the great agrarians Arthur Young and William Cobbett were later to make "pilgrimages."[2] In 1733, ailing and irritable, Tull published his *Horse-hoing Husbandry, or an Essay on the Principles of Tillage and Vegetation*,[3] a book outlining many new methods of farming which were to become commonplace in English agriculture by the end of the eighteenth century. The first principle of Tullian farming was the substitution, for ancient broadcast planting, of a drill husbandry for the planting of seed in rows. A plow for doing such planting, Tull had designed as early as 1701. Cobbett, explaining that by the old-fashioned system of broadcast planting one cabbage would grow to enormous size while hundreds around were starved and dwarfed, described Tull's system of drill husbandry as radical and democratic, all cabbages and more cabbages attaining a good size.[4] An important corollary for drill planting in Tull's system was horse-hoe cultivation, to eliminate weeds and pulverize the soil between the planted rows. Tullian methods of husbandry made their way gradually into English farming,[5] partly upon the not viewless wings of Robert Dodsley's poem "Agricul-

1. Marjorie Nicolson and Nora M. Mohler, "The Scientific Background of Swift's *Voyage to Laputa*," *Annals of Science*, II (1937), 330 ff.
2. *Rural Rides*, I, 36.
3. A specimen of this work, *Horse-hoing Husbandry*, was published in 1731.
4. *Rural Rides*, I, 28.
5. See *Gent. Mag.*, XXXIV (1764), 522 ff.

ture" (1753),[6] addressed to the Prince of Wales, in which Tull's ideas are wholly endorsed save for the restrictions placed on the use of manure. The poet points to the rich fields in the region of London and asks, with emotion,

> On Culture's hand
> Alone, do these Horticulists rely?
> Or do they owe to London's rich manure
> Those products which its crowded markets fill?[7]

Next to Tull, perhaps the best-known figure among the early improvers is Lord Townshend, who, having quarreled with his brother-in-law Robert Walpole, retired in 1730 from politics to live at his estate of Raynham in Norfolk and practice agriculture. The peer of the realm who chose to be an active farmer was an object of society's anxiety. At Raynham, as well as experimenting with Tullian methods, Townshend developed field turnip for use as a winter feed for cattle. Pope thereupon nicknamed him "Turnip Townshend." Field turnip very soon took their place in the improved rotations of the day, which also included the important grasses, clover and alfalfa (lucerne). Townshend's progressive ways of husbandry were copied by neighboring gentlemen in Norfolk, and Norfolk became in the middle years of the eighteenth century the best-farmed county in England, giving its name to this new scientific husbandry more properly called Tullian.[8] The value of land in that county increased tenfold between 1730 and 1760.

The eighteenth century saw many kinds of improvement in agriculture—invention of implements, new methods of fertilization, new systems of drainage. Mr. C. S. Orwin, who writes on agriculture in *Johnson's England*,[9] considers the most important feature of the agricultural revolution to be the work done by Robert Bakewell (1725–95) in the improvement of cattle. As a result principally of Bakewell's experiments with in-breeding, the weight and size of English cattle and sheep were nearly tripled in the eighteenth century. Bakewell's native Leicestershire became in this period the great cattle-raising county of England. Though this scientist has lain in a neglected and damaged grave at Dishley Grange,[1] he was in his own age so famous that Russian princes, German dukes, and travelers from all countries beat a path to his door.

In the decade of 1760 to 1770 the new farming became a matter for general and public notice. Arthur Young in 1770 said that more good

6. *Public Virtue*, Bk. I.   7. *Idem*, p. 36.
8. See *Gent. Mag.*, XXII (1752), 453 ff.
9. *Johnson's England*, A. S. Turberville, ed. (Oxford, Clarendon Press, 1933. 2 vols.), I, 261–99. Livestock was quite neglected in the seventeenth century when there were stirrings in other fields of agriculture. See Lord Ernle, "The Agricultural Revolution in England," *Encyclopaedia of the Social Sciences*, I, 580.
1. C. R. Fay, *Great Britain from Adam Smith to the Present Day* (London, Longmans, Green, 1928), p. 237.

sense had been shown in agriculture in the last ten years than in the hundred preceding ones.[2] We find the movement now taking its place in the pages of the *Gentleman's Magazine,* which carries articles on new methods in agriculture in its issues of December, 1763; January, February, March, May, June, July, August, September, October, November, and December, 1764; January, February, and April, 1765. It was in this decade that Arthur Young, having failed himself with the management of farms, came forth now as a writer on the new agriculture,[3] which was to be the passion of his life. With the fervor of a Wesley he rode through England and Ireland, and on the Continent, surveying farming, looking for new methods and criticizing the old. He was agriculture's bulldog.[4] He published accounts of his travels. He edited the important *Annals of Agriculture* which filled forty-six volumes between 1784 and 1815. He was largely responsible for the formation in 1793 of the Board of Agriculture, of which he became secretary, supervising the rather hastily prepared surveys of the agriculture of the counties of Great Britain which appeared from 1794 on.[5]

Young was perhaps more responsible than anyone else for making the profitable character of farming conducted by the new methods apparent to men of large estates, who were the first to appropriate the improvements of the experimenters. Of the great cultivators, the best known is probably that attractive figure Coke of Holkham in Norfolk, later Lord Leicester, whose character has been presented recently in an essay by Wallace Notestein.[6] When Coke came into his estate of more than 30,000 acres in 1776, it was bringing in an annual revenue of only about £2,000. Its cultivation at that time, according to Lady Townshend, consisted of "one blade of grass, and two rabbits fighting for that." But

2. Toynbee, p. 45.
3. See for bibliography G. D. Amery, "The Writings of Arthur Young," *Journal of the Royal Agricultural Society of England,* LXXXV (1924), 175–205.
4. As early as 1784 Young was calling for professorships of agriculture in Oxford and Cambridge, which have been neglectful of "young men whose residence is to be in the country," permitting them to leave the university with their adolescent view that country life means only horses and hounds. In proper agricultural seminaries they should be given a relish for the philosophical side of agriculture and a knowledge of all the new improvements. To this end Young suggests that three or four colleges in the two Universities be refashioned as agricultural schools and a tract of land be provided halfway between the Universities, to which students from each could repair for study. *Annals,* I, 78 ff. The Universities hardly fulfilled Young's dream. Edinburgh seems to be the first university to have had courses in agriculture, a graduate, Mr. Pulteney, having endowed a professorship to begin in June of 1789. *Idem,* XII, 483–6. A Dr. Walker was mentioned for the chair. *Idem,* XIV (1790), 131. In 1796 Dr. John Sibthorp, professor of botany in Oxford, created the Sherardian professorship of botany in Oxford, with the stipulation that the incumbent read lectures in rural economy. Arthur Young speaks of this as the first prospect of a professorship in agriculture in either of the Universities. *Idem,* XXVI (1796), 173–4.
5. See *idem,* XXI (1793), 129–50.
6. Wallace Notestein, *English Folk; a Book of Characters* (New York, Harcourt, Brace, 1938), pp. 51–71.

eventually this estate was yielding an income estimated at £20,000 to £30,000. This tenfold increase was the result of Coke's applying new agriculture to those lands he worked himself and popularizing these methods among his progressive tenant farmers. In Holkham Park he erected a column properly memorializing the work of the experimenters Tull and Bakewell. At the four corners of the monument were the following figures and inscriptions: a drilling machine with "The improvement of Agriculture," a cow with "'Breeding in all its branches," four sheep and a lamb with "Small in size but great in value," a plow with the words "Live and let live."[7] There were no cattle on the estate Coke inherited in 1776. With the aid of Bakewell and the duke of Bedford he learned to judge cattle and stocked his lands. Eight hundred starved Norfolk sheep were replaced with a fine flock of Southdowns. His fields, "inoculated" with sod, bore great crops of wheat and barley, the latter described as "hat-barley," so thick that it would hold a hat thrown on it. The turnips, which had been introduced in this county a generation before by Townshend, were raised in quantities at Holkham as a winter fodder for cattle.

> Some counties vaunt themselves in pies,
> And some in meat excel,
> For turnips of enormous size
> Fair Norfolk bears the bell.

In 1778 Coke introduced annual sheepshearings at Holkham, which eventually became world famous as agricultural fairs. The last of these exhibitions, held in 1821, was attended by more than seven hundred guests, among them Robert Owen, prophet to another age.[8]

Another great improver of this period was Francis Russell, fifth duke of Bedford (1765–1802). When he died, a young man, in 1802, the *Annals of Agriculture* wrote: "The agricultural world never, perhaps, sustained a greater individual loss than the husbandry of this empire has suffered by the death of the Duke of Bedford."[9] The *Annals* printed extracts from the funeral sermon preached at Woburn by the Reverend Edmund Cartwright, poet, inventor of the power loom, and improver. His text was "He cometh forth as a flower . . ."[1] The Bath and West of England Agricultural Society at this time proposed that a gold medallion of twenty guineas, with the head of Bedford and an allegorical design, be offered annually for the outstanding improvement in agricul-

---

7. Fay, *Great Britain from Adam Smith to the Present Day*, p. 238.
8. See *The Life of Robert Owen, Written by Himself* (London, 1857–58. 2 vols.), I, 218 ff.
9. *Annals*, xxxviii (1802), 369.
1. *Idem*, p. 385. Cartwright, though a minister, took a keen interest in the new agriculture. His funeral sermon on Bedford was censured as "improper from a clergyman." See *DNB*, under Cartwright.

ture.[2] The duke of Bedford had taken over his family estates in 1787. Ten years later the first sheepshearing was held at Woburn, to be continued "every succeeding year, but with greater increasing numbers and eclat, till it became at last by far the most respectable agricultural meeting ever seen in England; that is, in the world: attended by nobility, gentry, farmers, and graziers, from various parts of the three kingdoms; from many countries in Europe, and also from America." Bedford had great plans for agriculture. Manager himself of a modern farm and member of the newly formed Board of Agriculture (1793), he was especially interested in agricultural education.[3]

Other titled improvers were Turner's patron the earl of Egremont, a member of the Board of Agriculture who made his estate at Petworth a "college" of agriculture; the marquis of Rockingham who had the cultivation of 2,000 acres under his own supervision; the earl of Orford; the marquis of Stafford; Lord Clare in Essex; Lord Cathcart; and Lord Halifax. By 1780 there was said to be a general rage for farming throughout the kingdom. Agriculture took the place of rural sports and gardening in the country gentleman's life.[4] As Mantoux has said, the seventeenth-century cavalier was succeeded by the gentleman farmer.[5] And great ladies were not unaware of this activity, for in the *Annals of Agriculture* of 1786 we read that Lady Coventry was amusing herself with the management of her farm.[6] In observing the devotion of the great to agriculture, one may not overlook the king himself, "Farmer George." "The King's favour is as dew upon the grass." When the Great Park at Windsor became a royal possession in 1791, His Majesty undertook to convert it into a model progressive farm, 1,000 acres becoming a "Norfolk Farm" and 400 acres a "Flemish Farm." Here George experimented in the use of oxen, which were discovered to perform best with a five-day week.[7] Their superiority to horses was demonstrated against better, if less regal, contemporary authority. Kew Gardens would seem likewise to have been dedicated to horticulture. It was George who helped introduce into England, Merino sheep, excellent for wool, and in 1792 we see in the *Annals of Agriculture* an engraving of "Don," a Merino lamb with wonderful curling horns, given by His Majesty to Arthur Young. "How many millions of men are there," writes the editor, "that would smile, if I were to mention the sovereign of a great empire giving a ram to a farmer . . ."[8]

The enthusiasm of the lesser squire and country gentleman for the new agriculture expressed itself in agricultural societies which were a phenomenon of the late eighteenth century. "The end of the eighteenth

2. *Annals,* xxxviii (1802), 467.
3. See *idem,* pp. 369–73.
4. See Curtler, p. 193.
5. Mantoux, p. 165.
6. vi (1786), 126–7.
7. *Georgical Essays,* Alexander Hunter, ed. (York, 1803–4. 6 vols.), iv, 172–88.
8. *Annals,* xvii (1792), 529.

and beginning of the nineteenth centuries saw the establishment all over England of farmers' clubs, cattle shows, and ploughing matches."[9] It is interesting to note that the Kendal Agricultural Society was founded in 1799, the year of Wordsworth's return to the Lake country.[1] Meetings of these societies, generally quarterly, were usually held at noon at inns. The gatherings had their light side. There is "inside evidence" for supposing that the bottle circulated freely, that there was convivial conversation and a good deal of "three times three."[2] But papers were read, and some societies published their transactions. Their promotion of agriculture was accomplished mainly through premiums. Of these, there appear to have been two kinds. First, rewards in the form of silver cups or medals, given to fellow gentlemen for a gentlemanly attainment in agriculture, such as raising the finest ram or draining the most land. Then the societies offered cash prizes to small farmers and laborers for such an accomplishment as proficiency in plowing.[3] Landlord, tenant, and laborer were all encouraged in improvement by a premium system carried out on a generous scale. The wealthier agricultural societies, such as that of Sussex where the king was a member, were probably among the principal patrons of Georgian silversmiths. Even the small Kendal Society was spending £40 a year for silver cups.[4]

A goodly part of the membership of every agricultural society seems to have been made up of clergymen. We know in part what the eighteenth-century Anglican clergy were doing: they were improving the agriculture of England, perhaps with some eye to tithes. Of the 119 members of the Odiham Agricultural Society in 1785, 28 were clergymen![5] Most conspicuous of the Church of England's agrarians perhaps is Richard Watson (1737–1816), bishop of Llandaff, with whom Wordsworth had at least one encounter. Having become professor of chemistry at Cambridge without any previous study of this subject, and thereafter professor of divinity with somewhat similar preparation,[6] in 1782 Wat-

---

9. Curtler, p. 233. Henry Hamilton says that agricultural societies were springing up like mushrooms in Scotland in the seventies and after. Hamilton, p. 45. So far as I know there is no satisfactory account of these societies which played important economic and social parts in late eighteenth-century life. (But see Lord Ernle, *English Farming Past and Present* [3d ed. London, Longmans, Green, 1922], p. 209.) My notes include the names of about fifty such societies.

1. *Annals,* XXXVIII (1802), 473.   2. *Idem,* p. 179.

3. See the account in *idem* of the plowing matches sponsored by a club of farmers in Alloa, Clackmananshire, Scotland (XXIX [1797], 329–33). Each contestant plowed two ridges, to be examined by the judges after all had left the field. Banquets had formerly been furnished the plowmen following these contests, but there was so much arguing among contestants that the custom was dropped. Instead, the plowman now "gets a good sixpenny mutton-pie and a dram, and takes his horses home without delay." The first prize consisted of 15s., together with a silver medal worth the same amount. So successful had the contests been in Alloa that Clackmananshire was said to have fields that looked like gardens.

4. *Idem,* XXXVIII (1802), 474.   5. *Idem,* III (1785), 311–14.
6. *DNB.*

son was most properly consecrated bishop of Llandaff. He held in all some sixteen livings. Shortly after his consecration he moved to the sweet shores of Windermere in the Lake country, there building Calgarth House where Scott was to be a guest. His diocese, he visited every three years. The ambition of this Anglican bishop was "to be remembered as an improver of land and a planter of trees."[7] In the *Annals of Agriculture* Watson is reverently spoken of as that ardent improver who has imported Bakewell's sheep into Westmorland and who now is exhibiting the value of potatoes as a crop. "His Lordship appears to be an anxious and attentive farmer, is busily engaged in clearing and improving his new estate upon the Lake . . ."[8] To the *Annals of Agriculture* Watson was a hero. The bishop became a writer on agriculture, contributing to the *Georgical Essays* two articles on his favorite subject, the planting of trees,[9] proposing among other things that the tops of the mountains, useless for crops or pasture, be set with larches. With careful statistics he demonstrated that 1,000 acres so planted would in 60 years' time yield a profit of £114,400. Wordsworth, we may note, resented the planting of unlovely, fast-growing larches in the Lake country:[1] the poet, moreover, was said to have sneered at the bishop's "vegetable manufactory."[2]

By the last decades of the eighteenth century English farming was the wonder of the world. ". . . England has opened the eyes of other nations," wrote Don Joseph Valcarcel of Valencia.[3] The Abbé Millot in his *Elements of the History of England* spoke of this country as having brought agriculture to perfection.[4] The French published writings on farming under the title "Le Cultivateur anglais." The empress of Russia sent young men to England to study agriculture.[5] And poor Prince Lee Boo, who came to England with Captain Wilson only to die there of smallpox in 1784, had made his journey to learn the new methods of agriculture.[6]

7. D. C. Somervell, *English Thought in the Nineteenth Century* (New York, Longmans, Green, 1938), p. 17.
8. *Annals*, xx (1793), 2–6. 9. *Georgical Essays*, v (1804), 161–8, 169–76.
1. See *Letters . . . Middle Years*, II, 489.
2. *DNB*, under Watson. 3. *Annals*, xxiii (1795), 208 n.
4. See *Gent. Mag.*, xl (1770), 458. 5. *Annals*, ii (1784), 233–7; v (1786), 431.
6. H. N. Fairchild, *The Noble Savage* (New York, Columbia University Press, 1928), p. 115. It was a general belief in late eighteenth-century England that their age was responsible for the revival of agriculture. In the Cromwellian period there had been a proper regard for agriculture, and in Milton's "school" rural economics were given a principal place, his pupils being required to read Cato, Varro, and Columella. Cowley and, in a sense, Evelyn shared in this progressive seventeenth-century movement, though the latter is rather a lone advocate of agriculture in a later period that neglected it. When Evelyn's *Terra, or a Philosophical Discourse on Earth,* appeared in 1675, the spirit of the time was no longer rural. The Reverend W. Lamport, whose essay "On the Improvement of Agriculture," *Georgical Essays*, v (1804), 9–24, I am here following, comments: "A nation may be civilized to so high a degree of refinement, as that the politer part of its inhabitants will associate in cities and towns, and attend to nothing but pleasure

A certain not unfamiliar optimism, we may note, accompanied the remarkable developments of English agriculture. Wrote Robert Owen: "For man knows not the limit to his power of creating food. How much has this power been latterly increased in these islands! And in them such knowledge is in its infancy. Yet compare even this power of raising food with the efforts of the Bosgemens or other savages, and it will be found, perhaps, as one to a thousand."[7] Wrote Godwin: "The improvements to be made in cultivation, and the augmentations the earth is capable of receiving in the article of productiveness, cannot, as yet, be reduced to any limits of calculation."[8] The expectation of the productivity of agriculture and the proportions to which cattle might be brought was tremendous.[9] It was no small part of the cynicism of Malthus' *Essay on Population* that he defined the limits of expansion of this wonderful new agriculture, which, however remarkable, could not keep pace with the increase in population.[1]

It is interesting to consider for a moment eighteenth-century attitudes toward nature in the light of nature's doings. Never was the earth more fertile, more swollen with life. But despite increase and foison plenty, despite all this attention to the seed and growth of things, there seems to have been no tendency to revive the old Mediterranean view of nature, expressed in such a poem as Virgil's *Georgics*. Believing the "vitalized seed"[2] of the atom to be at the heart of things, Virgil saw nature as energy and he accordingly represented the earth as the great generative mother whose womb is warmed by the burning of grass, whose side is wounded by the plow. His procreative personification was politely ignored in an expansive agrarian period which nonetheless made the *Georgics* its favorite poem. The English mind preferred to find in nature, not vital energy, but rather natural law.

Upper-class enthusiasms for agriculture, as some remarks already have suggested, were not always the enthusiasms of the poetic mind. Wordsworth on one occasion did write that the landed gentleman should ". . . give countenance to improvements in agriculture, steering clear of the pedantry of it, and showing that its grossest utilities will connect

---

and the fine arts." Such was the age of Charles II. "At that period, the maxims of the celebrated Bacon, the example of Milton, the efforts of the Royal Society, the proposal of Cowley, the complaint of Evelyn, and his just observations on the necessity of an enlarged education, in order to improve the lands of England, were exhibited in vain." But now in his own time (1804) Lamport is able to say, "agriculture hath arisen, like a star of the first magnitude, in our hemisphere . . ."

7. "New View of Society," *The Life of Robert Owen, Written by Himself*, I, 328.
8. William Godwin, *Enquiry Concerning Political Justice* (3d ed. London, 1798). 2 vols.), II, 518.
9. *Annals*, XXIX (1797), 267–8.
1. T. R. Malthus, *An Essay on the Principle of Population* (New ed., enlarged. London, 1803), pp. 360 ff.
2. See Tenney Frank, *Vergil* (New York, Henry Holt, 1922), p. 163.

themselves harmoniously with the more intellectual arts, and even thrive
the best under such connection . . ."[3] His attitude toward the new
agriculture seems in another instance, however, to have been one of mild
amusement and indifference. This is his tone in that most familiar
"Epistle" of 1811, addressed to Sir George Beaumont from a rude,
unplastered seaside fortress on the southwest coast of Cumberland where
he had taken two of his children for their health. Diversions are few:
he cannot paint or play the flute, and so he occupies himself with his
homely muse. Across the way lies Mona Isle, daily seen. But what goes
on there, he does not know.

> Ask not of me, whose tongue can best appease
> The mighty tumults of the HOUSE OF KEYS;
> The last year's cup whose Ram or Heifer gained,
> What slopes are planted, or what mosses drained . . .[4]

The Leicestershire Improved Breed

Others were similarly amused. An anonymous poem, *The Pursuits of
Agriculture* (1810), satirized the optimism, pedantry, and general
Laputan nonsense of the agricultural experimenters.[5] This poem should
have satisfied a reviewer of James Grahame's *British Georgics* (1809),
who called for a satire on the "Medal-and-Cup men, who pride themselves upon growing tallow instead of meat . . . who instead of 'marry-
ing the vine to the elm,' negociate [sic] the meetings of their tups and
ewes, and enact the part of 'Sir Pandarus of Troy' for a favourite bull."[6]
Bewick, the wood engraver, had his own experience with the cattle
breeders. As an artist he was requested by these "fat cattle makers"
to do pictures of their prize cattle which would exaggerate their size,
showing them as monstrously big. Bewick refused to over-draw for
them, though he says many artists were subservient to such wishes.[7]

3. *Early Letters*, p. 525.
4. Ll. 65–8. Wordsworth, *Poetical Works*, pp. 521–5.
5. Reviewed in *Quarterly Review*, III (1810), 374–9.
6. *Idem*, III (1810), 461.   7. *Memoir*, pp. 183–4.

2. *The Gentleman Farmer*

Even as we shall observe the development of the cult of the peasant in the later years of the eighteenth century, we shall also note the parallel creation of a cult of the country gentleman. In nature's country house were many mansions. It is, to be sure, in the literature closely associated with agricultural improvement in England that we find frequent expression of the sentiment that life in the country is an ideal most proper for a gentleman.[8] In the language of the precise Lockian psychology of his age, Lord Kames, writing in 1776, thus spoke to the gentlemen of Scotland of the virtues belonging to country life:

But what I chiefly insist on is, that laying aside irregular appetites and ambitious views, agriculture is of all occupations the most consonant to our nature; and the most productive of contentment, the sweetest sort of happiness. In the first place, it requires that moderate degree of exercise, which corresponds the most to the ordinary succession of our perceptions. Fox-hunting produces a succession too rapid; angling produces a succession too slow. Agriculture corresponds not only more to the ordinary succession, but has the following signal property, that a farmer can direct his operations with that degree of quickness and variety which is agreeable to his own train of perceptions. In the next place, to every occupation that can give a lasting relish, hope and fear are essential. A fowler has little enjoyment in his gun who misses frequently; and he loses all enjoyment, when every shot is death: a poacher, so dextrous, may have pleasure in the profit, but none in the art. The hope and fears that attend agriculture, keep the mind always awake, and in an enlivening degree of agitation. Hope never approaches certainty so near, as to produce security; nor is fear ever so great, as to create deep anxiety and distress. Hence it is, that a gentleman farmer tolerably skilful, never tires of his work; but is as keen the last moment as the first. Can any other employment compare with farming in that respect? In the third place, no other occupation rivals agriculture, in connecting private interest with that of the public. How pleasing to think, that every step a man makes for his own good, promotes that of his country! Even where the balance happens to turn against the farmer, he has still the comfort that his country profits by him. Every gentleman farmer must of course be a patriot; for patriotism, like other virtues, is improved and fortified by exercise. In fact, if there be any remaining patriotism in a nation, it is found among that class of men.[9]

These observations appeared in the preface of a treatise on practical agriculture, *The Gentleman Farmer,* addressed to a gentry of Scotland who currently were showing themselves even as active as their English fellows in improving their agriculture.

8. The relation of the moral ideal of ruralism to those practical developments in agriculture we have just been discussing is the theme of an excellent recent essay by Paul H. Johnstone, entitled "Turnips and Romanticism" and published in *Agricultural History*, XII (1938), 224–55.
9. *The Gentleman Farmer* (5th ed. Edinburgh, 1802), pp. xvii–xviii.

In 1784 Arthur Young published an essay of some length, entitled "On the Pleasures of Agriculture."[1] His remarks, addressed to gentlemen, are introduced with quotations from Cicero and Cowley: "Venio nunc ad voluptates agricolarum"; "We may talk what we please of lilies and lions rampant, and spread eagles in fields d'or or d'argent; but if heraldry were guided by reason, a plough in a field arable would be the most noble and antient arms." In praising rural life Young represents it as free from the anxiety which marks the life in commerce and industry. And, further, its pleasures are lasting. It does not fail one with the years. In fact, one might say, agriculture begins at forty. "When the evening of life approaches, wrapped in clouds, in darkness, and in uncertainty, it is then our pleasures are brought to the test; and we have an undeceiving criterion to judge of our pursuits."[2] Agriculture, moreover, provides intellectual interests sufficient for a man, as Xenophon, Cicero, Virgil, and Horace all have declared. Modern farming especially engages the mind, Young says, since botany, chemistry, and mineralogy are all a part of its science. Thus agriculture is interpreted by Arthur Young as offering the gentleman a life at once active and intellectual, exciting yet calm. This essay appeared in the second volume of the great periodical of practical agriculture begun under Young's own editorship in 1784.

In such ideal pictures as these of gentlemanly country life we recognize one prevailing spirit—the spirit of classicism and the golden mean. Indeed, not only was such ruralism classical in spirit: it likewise had strong classical sources, and these principally Roman—in Cato, Virgil, Horace, and Cicero, and in Strabo, Varro, and Columella. The Greeks, one eighteenth-century writer felt, were city people, contemptuous of the country; the Romans, on the contrary, had a proper awareness of the values of the rural life.[3] English agrarians were clearly conscious that they were doing outside Rome what the Romans did, namely, farm. Examples are numerous. Walter Harte in the first of his *Essays on Husbandry* (1764), which is something of a eulogy of agriculture, cites countless ancient writers to prove the dignity of farming, but particularly he quotes the Roman writers, and especially Virgil: "Non ullus aratro dignus honos."[4] Sir John Sinclair, "High Priest of Ceres," prints at the head of his presidential address to the Board of Agriculture (May 24, 1796) the Latin of Pliny: "Igitur et de cultura agri praecipere, principale fuit, etiam apud exteros . . ."[5] This ruralism which accom-

1. *Annals*, II, 456–87.   2. *Idem*, p. 466.
3. Dr. William Falconer, *Remarks on the Influence of Climate, Situation, Nature of Country, Population, Nature of Food, and Way of Life on the Disposition and Temper, Manners and Behaviour, Intellects, Laws and Customs, Form of Government, and Religion, of Mankind* (London, 1781), pp. 356 ff. For the rural sentiment of the classical tradition, see Paul H. Johnstone, "In Praise of Husbandry," *Agricultural History*, XI (1937), 80–95.   4. P. 5.
5. *Annals*, XXVI (1796), 504. The Romans had little to teach the English about the

panied agricultural improvement, far from being a break with classicism, was simply a redirection and extension of the Augustan spirit of the eighteenth century. A gentleman did not have to change his library when he moved from Pope's London to his estate in Norfolk.

3. Enclosure of Open Fields

There is some irony in the improvers' praise of rural life, for in England improvement led inevitably to the enclosures which did so much to bring an end to rural living for that part of the population which probably derived most benefit from a life on the land—the yeomen, the small farmers, and the country laborers. First came the enclosure of open field villages, and later the enclosure of commons. Let us consider for a moment the former and its effects.

To understand why improvers should want such enclosure we must recall for a moment the structure of the ancient open village,[6] specimens of which survive as novelties in our own time. A manor house, set apart by itself, and a group of farmers' and laborers' tenements clustered together along a street comprised the dwellings of the typical village. The village lands might conveniently be considered to be of three kinds —first, strips of arable; then, somewhat more extensive fields of enclosed pasture; and, finally, a large tract of waste, or "commons." But all the lands of the village were in a sense common land, for they were held in a communal way by the lord of the manor and his villagers. Each village farmer through his lease from the manor had title to some strips in the arable fields, and also with his lease went rights to put to pasture in the enclosed meadows a certain number of cattle, the number being originally limited to the cattle necessary for the cultivation of his arable holdings. However, there seems to have been a tendency toward unlimited pasturage in many villages; and these overcrowded common pastures, which gave but a poor livelihood to cattle, became in the eighteenth century an argument on the side of the enclosers. The village

---

actual practice of agriculture. Their agriculture had improved little upon the oldest methods of the ancient world. Rotations were bad; tools were clumsy; their plow a rude instrument which dug but did not turn the earth. There was negligence in applying manure and in selecting seed. Superstition controlled a calendar of lucky days and also affected breeding practices. See, for instance, *Encyclopaedia of the Social Sciences*, I, 575.

6. See "Manor," *Dict. Pol. Econ.* Also see Gonner, pp. 3–17.

farmer also had rights in the third section of the village lands, the waste or commons, rights of estovers and of turbary permitting him to take certain amounts of wood and peat. Just as the villager's rights were vested in these common fields of arable, pasture, and waste, so were those of the lord of the manor, however much greater his holdings might be: "his demesne lay largely in the open fields, and was subject to the rules that regulated the cultivation of those fields."

The disadvantages of such tenure for a progressive landlord who wanted to apply the new methods of farming and had the capital to do so have been recognized by all historians of the enclosure movement. Time wasted in working small divided fields, the pointlessness of using the new methods of drainage and fertilization on fields that often rotated through the village holders, the difficulty of breeding good cattle when they were pastured with the village stock to be starved and corrupted by the common herd, the obstacles to using the new rotations—these and many more considerations prompted the eighteenth-century landlord to try to consolidate his arable fields and pasture.

Though the wealthy improver desired these changes, the small farmer preferred the system of open fields and common pasture. For him there were many advantages in a system of communal farming. The village was able to employ certain common officials, such as viewer of fields, shepherd, swineherd, cowherd, hayward, or pinder. Such cooperative features of the community seemed less feasible if every man were to hold and work his own piece of land. And if the small farmer was *owner* of his lands, enclosure cost him dearly in the expense of the act itself, his contribution for the new roads, and the expense of fencing a small property, always greater in proportion than for larger holdings. The cost of such fencing was perhaps only £5, but in a time when domestic industries were on the decline, this expenditure was sometimes just enough to make many a small owner decide to sell his land and move to the city.

The small farmer was sufficiently aware of the effect of enclosure to oppose the movement. Facing enclosures in the open village of Raunds in Northamptonshire, the small proprietors of this community thus petitioned parliament in 1797:

. . . and they further conceive, that a more ruinous Effect of this Inclosure will be the almost total Depopulation of their Town, now filled with bold and hardy Husbandmen, from among whom, and the Inhabitants of other open Parishes, the Nation has hitherto derived its greatest Strength and Glory, in the Supply of its Fleets and Armies, and driving them, from Necessity and Want of Employ, in vast Crowds, into manufacturing Towns, where the very Nature of their Employment, over the Loom or the Forge, soon may waste their Strength, and consequently debilitate their Posterity, and by imperceptible Degrees obliterate that great Principle of Obedience to the Laws of

God and their Country, which forms the Character of the simple and artless
Villagers, more equally distributed through the Open Countries, and on
which so much depends the good Order and Government of the State . . .[7]

Prior to the eighteenth century there had been some voluntary enclosure by "suffrance, approvement, and agreement." Mr. H. L. Gray,
author of *English Field Systems,* is inclined to regard the entire movement as a progressive process beginning far back in the history of English agriculture,[8] coming to its climax in the eighteenth century. This
century, however, saw the rise of a somewhat more arbitrary kind of
enclosure by way of private acts in parliament, reflecting new parliamentary power.[9] From 1700 to 1760, 237,845 acres, mostly arable, were
enclosed as a result of 152 such parliamentary acts of enclosure. From
1761 to 1801, 2,428,721 acres were enclosed through 1,479 parliamentary acts, while between 1802 and 1844, 1,075 acts enclosed 1,610,302
acres.[1] In 1801 a general enclosure bill, strongly supported by the new
Board of Agriculture, was passed to facilitate and cheapen the entire
procedure. Open village systems had prevailed principally in the counties
from York south to Dorset, especially the Midland counties, and this
accordingly was the area of such enclosures. "The section of England
affected by the Acts relating to open fields lay almost entirely between
two lines, one drawn straight from Lyme Regis to Gloucester and from
Gloucester to the Tees estuary, the second straight from Southampton
to Lowestoft passing London a few miles to the west."[2]

That enclosure in the open villages was so harmful to the small farmers
was owing to the fact that it came at a time when the small rural household was meeting other economic embarrassments. The improved
methods of farming in themselves had been prejudicial to the small
farmer, for he could not afford to take advantage of them. Crops he
might rotate without expense, but other improvements were costly. It
took money to put marl on the soil, to drain land, to buy new agricultural implements, and to purchase thoroughbred cattle for improving
stock. Only the gentleman farmer could afford the "improvements."
And at the very time when the small farmer was feeling definite handi-
caps in practicing agriculture, he began to lose income from domestic
industry. Little of England's weaving, but most of her spinning, had

7. Quoted in Hammond, p. 15.
8. Gray points out how much voluntary enclosure there was. Gray, pp. 116, 149, 152.
See also Johnson, p. 92.
9. Gonner, p. 59.
1. Johnson, p. 90. Ernle writes: "Between 1760 and 1820 at least 4,000,000 acres of
common meadow, arable, and pasture were enclosed by acts of Parliament and redis-
tributed as farms in individual occupation, owners being awarded compact freehold
blocks equivalent in value to their scattered strips and common rights." *Encyclopaedia
of the Social Sciences,* I, 580.
2. Clapham, I, 19.

been done in the cottage.[3] Now, in the latter half of the eighteenth century, this industry was being transferred from the country home to the factory.

England's yeoman class, which had comprised a most substantial part of her population, is thought to have been very hard hit during these last years of the eighteenth century. Since 1429 it had been the great voting population. Indeed, the rise of this class had told in no small part the story of democracy in England. The term "yeoman"[4] is used loosely to describe all small farmers, but a sufficiently liberal definition of the term is one that includes two classes of proprietors: (a) freeholders and (b) copyholders or customary tenants. The freeholders were originally the villeins of the feudal manor who became free tenants after Domesday when their services were commuted to rent.[5] By statute of 1290 this rent was fixed in perpetuity, so that the heir to a holding had to make "only such feudal payments for his land as had been settled before the year 1290."[6] With the fall in the value of money and the rise in the worth of land these rents became in time only nominal "quit rents." In time also the oath of fealty to the lord of the manor became obsolete, feudal courts lost their importance, and the restrictions on the willing of freehold property were removed. The freeholder could properly be spoken of as "full proprietor of his land."[7]

A second large body of yeomen consisted of copyholders, or customary tenants, a class of owners whose titles were restricted in ways that the free tenants' were not. In the case of copyhold tenure, here again time modified in many instances the features of the medieval contract, and "Thus tenure by copyhold became merely a form of landownership, without any servile taint."[8] "In the point of service a man can scarce discern any difference between freehold lands and copyhold lands."[9] But this tenure seems to have kept in certain instances many servile features, and this was the case in Cumberland and Westmorland where most of the land was held by copyhold or customary tenure.

By 1800, we are told by Toynbee, the 180,000 small *freeholders* who made up about one-sixth of the population of England in 1700 had practically disappeared. The process of extinction was very rapid, he says, after 1760.[1] A more recent historian takes a soberer view. Clapham,[2] admitting the difficulty of getting any clear picture of the true situation, argues against the notion of any catastrophic decline of

3. See, for instance, G. D. H. Cole, "Town-Life in the Provinces," *Johnson's England,* I, 199.
4. See "Yeomen," *Dict. Pol. Econ.*   5. See "Manor," *idem.*
6. See "Freehold," *idem.*   7. *Ibid.*
8. W. S. Holdsworth, *An Historical Introduction to the Land Law* (Oxford, Clarendon Press, 1927), p. 44.
9. Coke, as quoted by Holdsworth, *idem,* pp. 44–5.
1. Toynbee, p. 59.   2. Clapham, Vol. I, Bk. I, chap. iv.

English yeomanry in this period. However, one recognizes some tendency in Clapham's account to cite as authority the improvers themselves,
such as Eden and Sinclair, and also the *General Surveys* published under
the auspices of the Board of Agriculture. The improvers were not always
the first to recognize the effect of their developments upon the small
owners. Nonetheless, Clapham's judgment of the facts of small ownership is a good corrective for the sweeping impressions we derive from
Toynbee and others. But Clapham cites as "the most cautious and judicial
modern student"[3] of the subject, Gonner, author of *Common Land and
Inclosure,* and these are Gonner's words:

> With these causes in operation there is little room for wonder at the steady
> and widespread disappearance of the small farmer, and especially of the small
> owner cultivating his own little farm. The fact itself is beyond all doubt. From
> all quarters comes the complaint; and even those who rejoiced in the techni-
> cal improvement in agriculture were constrained to join in the dirge over the
> yeoman farmer.[4]

Clapham finds much more evidence for the decline in this period of
the small farmers who were not owners. He supposes that only too
frequently their leases were not renewed, and he conjectures that much
of the lamentation for the disappearance of the yeomanry was in reality
a lament for this class of small farmers, whose long leases and security
had in many cases entitled them to the dignity of freeholders. The small
tenant farmer was adversely affected by the great developments in this
age of "liberty and cultivation." He did not, like the small owner, have
the expense of road-building and fencing brought by enclosure, but he
met the same difficulties in transferring his economy from corporate
village farming to individual farming. He suffered similarly from loss
of domestic industry and from the rather prohibitive cost of the improvements in farming necessary if he were to compete with the great
producers. But what affected the small tenant farmer most severely was
the rise in rents. Landlords could command bigger rents for land that
could be made so much more productive by the new methods of farming,
especially at a time when England's population was increasing so
rapidly.

Large capitalistic farms are a phenomenon of the last years of the
eighteenth century. As early as 1758 a writer in the *Gentleman's Magazine* spoke of the disappearance of small farms in parishes of Suffolk
and Norfolk. Where thirty years before there had been fourteen, fifteen,
or sixteen farmers in a parish, there were now but three or two or even
only one.[5] Thomas Wright stated in 1779 that twenty-four farms of
50 to 150 acres in several Hertfordshire parishes had been consolidated

3. *Idem,* I, 116.   4. Gonner, p. 369.
5. *Gent. Mag.,* xxviii (1758), 509–10.

into three farms.[6] In 1795 Eden found in a village in Dorsetshire two farms where twenty years before there had been thirty.[7] Somewhat later Cobbett came across a farmer in the north of Hampshire who was holding land that formerly constituted forty farms.[8] Coke of Holkham is quoted by Marx as saying: "It is a melancholy thing to stand alone in one's country. I look around and not a house is to be seen but mine. I am the giant of Giant Castle, and have eat up all my neighbours."[9]

If the improving movement with its enclosure did not destroy small ownership and small farming quite so thoroughly as some have supposed, it was not altogether from want of will on the part of the improvers, for by their own testimony they were opposed to small farming of any kind. In page after page of the writings of the progressive farmers one is told that the small farmer is not an improver. He is conservative, unprogressive, in fact, in the words of La Fleur, "la bête la plus opiniâtré du monde."[1] "The poor farmer is always a bad one." Wight's comments on the tenants of Scotland, written in 1778, summarize the general backwardness which was said to characterize all small operators on the soil.

Their spirits are depressed by poverty; and they have neither activity or knowledge to cultivate their lands in any good manner. They languidly go on in the old beaten track; and it never enters their thoughts that there is a better method. We need but except the fields round towns and one or two shires to make this picture suit all the husbandmen of Scotland.[2]

Aiton, surveying the agriculture of Ayrshire, says sarcastically of the small farmers of Scotland: "An extensive acquaintance with the mysterious, abstruse and disputed points of systematic divinity, was the species of knowledge they generally sought after, and to which the greatest fame was attached."[3] Again, in the *Annals of Agriculture* we read that it is vain to expect improvements from "uneducated, that is, from little farmers. . . ."; ". . . if gentlemen, and the great occupiers, with modern ideas, by their attention to the subject, do not improve it, experience tells us it will never be improved at all."[4] These are typical of the comments issuing from the improving mind on the subject of small farming.

If land were not improved, the same group argued, there would be

6. Quoted in Karl Marx, *Capital,* Frederick Engels, ed. (New York, Modern Library, n.d.), p. 797.   7. See Toynbee, p. 89.
8. *Rural Rides,* I, 30.   9. *Capital,* p. 762, n. 1.
1. *Annals,* VI (1786), 12. Malthus said a professor at Copenhagen told him the reason for the backwardness of Norway's agriculture was the want of gentleman farmers to set examples and break the routine and prejudice in conduct of farms carried down through generations. *An Essay on the Principle of Population,* p. 193.
2. Andrew Wight, quoted in Hamilton, p. 41.
3. William Aiton, quoted in *idem,* pp. 41-2.
4. *Annals,* XXI (1793), 231.

just that much less food to support human beings. The big agriculturists took to their side the argument from population. They reasoned that large-scale agriculture, using the new methods and also a division of labor unsuitable to small-scale cultivating,[5] though it might decrease the relative numbers engaged in agriculture, would nevertheless augment the supply of food to support a larger general population. The population argument in support of large, progressive farming, which one encounters everywhere, was an impressive one, and this is what must have made Shelley look upon agricultural improvements as activities worthy of the poet. In 1812 Shelley had gone to Tremadoc for a while, a little town built on land reclaimed from the sea by a Mr. Madock, who "had the design to recover more land by building a great embankment nearly a mile long across the estuary which there runs in from the coast." Shelley was excited by the project, regarded it as "a piece of scientific philanthropy," and sought to raise money for it in Sussex and elsewhere.[6] About this time, too, the erstwhile radical, and still wealthy, Walter Savage Landor plunged into progressive agriculture on a tremendous scale, showed his usual impatience after a sudden enthusiasm, and left the project to be managed by his mother.[7] His intentions may have been similarly philanthropic.

The increased population supported by the surplus of improved agriculture would, however, be living in cities. Hence, many of the great enthusiasts for agriculture, who had so many pleasant things to say as well about the moral benefits of rural life, were obliged to become exponents of the big city. In an issue of the *Annals of Agriculture*[8] we hear Arthur Young disagreeing with Mirabeau's opinion that large cities are pernicious. He speaks also of the infinite importance of London and Paris as markets for the big farmer's surplus, a point repeated in another essay in the *Annals,* entitled "Importance of London to the National Husbandry."[9] For the *Annals* of 1790,[1] Signor Paolo Balsamo, professor of agriculture in the University of Palermo, writes from Sutton Hall his "Thoughts on Great Cities." The professor of agriculture defends the character of the city from the charge of the moralists and sees, as did every advanced thinker in agriculture, the importance of the city as a market for a flourishing agriculture. An increasing inconsistency appeared in the literature on progressive farming as the enthusiasts for the plow and country life became as well the advocates of the big city. The *Georgical Essays* print in 1803 an article of Arthur Young's, "On the Size of Farms,"[2] where he argues for large farms

---

5. *Idem,* VII (1786), 519.
6. A. Clutton-Brock, *Shelley. The Man and the Poet* (4th ed. London, Methuen, 1929), pp. 72 ff. Goethe's Faust, we will remember, found some satisfaction finally in the work of draining swamps.   7. *DNB.*
8. XII (1789), 471–7.   9. XXIII (1795), 271–3.
1. XIII (1790), 465–82.   2. *Georgical Essays,* IV (1803), 555–70.

on the basis of their superior productivity. Realizing that this means the elimination of many small farmers, Young is led to say, "Cultivation is not essential to the happiness of the individual . . ." What a statement to come from Arthur Young!

4. Enclosure of Commons

The improved methods of farming, by which land could be made many times more productive, made landlords anxious to extend as well as to consolidate their holdings. To add to his domain, the lord of the manor, often assisted in an enclosure move by the parish priest,[3] set

3. Sterne's activities are suggestive. He was an experimenter in the new methods of agriculture. His friend Charles Turner of Kirkleatham was regarded by Arthur Young as one of the leading authorities on farming. See *Letters of Laurence Sterne*, L. P. Curtis, ed. (Oxford, Clarendon Press, 1935), p. 382, n. 5. With his wife's fortune Sterne acquired lands, buying in 1744 a dairy farm and three other properties. As vicar of Sutton, he was the third local landholder, the first holders being Lord Fauconberg and Philip Harland. In the article on Sterne in *DNB* we read: "With characteristic disregard of the rights of his poor parishioners, he, in his capacity, not of clergyman, but of owner of land outside his glebe, actively supported Lord Fauconberg, the lord of the manor of Sutton, and his neighbour, Philip Harland, in securing the passage through parliament in 1756 of a private act 'for dividing and enclosing several fields, meadows, and commons in the township of Sutton upon the Forest.'" The land enclosed amounted to 3,000 acres. Sterne's own allotments were desirably situated and somewhat larger than was his due. Cross writes: "By the favors of his friends, Sterne was thus lifted into a small country squire who cultivated his lands and had cottages for his laborers." W. L. Cross, *Life and Times of Laurence Sterne* (3d ed. New Haven, Yale University Press, 1929), p. 113. Later the commons of Stillington, where Sterne was also vicar, were enclosed.

But at the very time Sterne was active in enclosing (a passion he was later to bequeath to the excited Mr. Shandy), he was losing his interest in practising agriculture, was in fact becoming disgusted with the business. In 1758 he resolved to lease his lands to be rid of the bother. Sterne's retirement from active farming gave him time, fortunately, for his career in literature. In 1767 (September 19), he wrote to a friend: "You are much to blame if you dig for marle, unless you are sure of it.—I was once such a puppy myself, as to pare, and burn, and had my labour for my pains, and two hundred pounds out of pocket.—Curse on farming (said I) I will try if the pen will not succeed better than the spade.—The following up of that affair (I mean farming) made me lose my temper, and a cart load of turneps [sic] was (I thought) very dear at two hundred pounds.—"

We should perhaps keep in mind Sterne the improver and the encloser when we read his account in the *Sentimental Journey* of the peasant love feast on Mount Taurira—a

about to annex that remarkable feudal institution, the commons, which since the time of Norman lawyers[4] had been recognized as his property. In defense of the enclosure of commons it may be said that the commons waste was used with neglect and carelessness, so that its productivity was only a fraction of what it might have been. The national interest, particularly with population on the rise as it was in the eighteenth century, required a more productive use of these large tracts of land. Bentham, who was not uninterested in the general happiness, approved of enclosure of such lands.

The actual use that had been made of commons waste cannot be stated too clearly. It figured somewhat, as we have seen, in the economy of the small owner and farmer, providing him with wood and fuel. (The rights these small husbandmen held by their lease in commons were supposedly to be recognized at an enclosure. Yet there is universal agreement again among historians that no proper equivalent was generally awarded such claimants.[5]) But it was for the laborer, the wage earner, the poor of the parish that this commons waste, this "commonage of nature," had had most significance. An occasional village laborer held rights in the arable and pasture lands, but the property rights of the great majority of day laborers, we may suppose, were represented in this large tract of waste. These rights were unwritten and hence unrecognized at enclosure, though the laborer's livelihood was in no small measure dependent upon the commons. Here he gathered his furze or wood for fire; here he kept a cow, a pig, some bees. Here he made his garden. Here, too, he housed the whole fairy world that haunted his imagination. Under certain conditions the laborer had even been allowed to erect his own cottage on the waste. Indeed, the commons had meant that the laborer was really not just a wage earner but a person with some property and therewith security. So, for Wordsworth's Simon Lee,[6] a laborer, his improvident youth did not spell ruin because he had the commons as a backlog. This little man, who once could outrun the horse and hound in hunting with the master of Ivor-Hall in Cardiganshire, had some social security in his decrepit old age. Living in a little mud hut on the commons, with a wife nearly as rickety as himself, he cultivated a scrap of land he had enclosed when he was younger and

---

family supper of lentil soup, wheaten loaves, and wine, followed by a dance with the old father playing the *vielle*. It was the dance that Sterne especially remembered, for it was both joyous and religious, a cheerful grace, as it were, coming at the end of the feast. Sterne's is an early contribution to the cult of the peasant, and a notable one, for we may see here perhaps a pagan reading of the peasant that is rare if not unique in his time.

4. See the article "Commons," *Encyclopaedia Britannica* (14th ed.), VI, 124 ff.

5. After enclosure one-quarter of the 379-acre waste of the parish of Winforton in Herefordshire went to 13 claimants to rights of common, the rest to the lord of the manor. Gray, pp. 149–50. Johnson says small landowners did not receive an equitable share of enclosed wastes. Johnson, p. 100.

6. Wordsworth, *Poetical Works*, p. 483.

stronger—a small piece, but one too big for him now to till. Here on the commons Wordsworth encountered Simon, trying to unearth a stump of (appropriately) rotten wood.

Between 1700 and 1844 there were 1,765,711 acres of commons waste enclosed by parliamentary act,[7] "stolen," to use Marx's verb, from the agricultural population of England. This enclosure movement, which affected the country generally, took on great momentum in the last years of the eighteenth century and was completed in the first half of the nineteenth. Hardy's uncultivated "Egdon Heath" was, as he tells us, an anomaly in the latter years of the nineteenth century. The Lake counties of Cumberland and Westmorland witnessed enclosure of commons rather late but rather fully, it would appear, for between 1820 and 1870 these counties led the country in the amount of waste enclosed.[8] The commons and wastes in the Lake District had been extensive. Pringle estimated in 1794 that three-fourths of Cumberland was uncultivated. These wastes were used for the common pasture of sheep during the summer months.[9] But those who surveyed the Lake counties for the Board of Agriculture were eager to have these lands converted into enclosed arable, restricted pasture, or tree plantations. Bailey, Pringle, Culley, and the bishop of Llandaff all saw the enclosure of these wide wastes as the first need of an improved agriculture in these districts. Hutchinson also became an advocate of enclosure, dedicating his massive History of the County of Cumberland (1794) rather ominously to Sir John Sinclair and the honorable members of the Board of Agriculture. It is interesting to know that Wordsworth was later to oppose single-handed the enclosure of the commons of Grasmere. And he won out, the commons remaining beautiful and the freemen keeping their rights of "foddering and goosage."[1]

The hardships of the laborer in the wake of the enclosure of the commons are, I think, generally acknowledged. Clapham is as explicit on this matter as the Hammonds. Having had good times through most of the century,[2] the laborer found himself in the 1790's in distressing circumstances. His condition, Toynbee says, became acute in the last years of the eighteenth century and continued so until 1834.[3] In the

7. Johnson, p. 90.   8. Clapham, I, 15.   9. See below, p. 92.

1. H. D. Rawnsley, "Reminiscences of Wordsworth among the Peasantry of Westmoreland," Wordsworthiana; a Selection from Papers Read to the Wordsworth Society, W. Knight, ed. (London, Macmillan, 1889), pp. 101–2. This is the reminiscence: "Well, well, he couldn't abear to see faäce o' things altered, ye kna. It was all along of him that Grasmere folks have their Common open. Ye may ga now reet up to sky over Grisedale, wi'out laying leg to fence, and all through him. He said it was a pity to enclose it and run walls over it, and the quality backed him, and he won. Folks was angry enough, and wrote rhymes about it; but why, why, it's a deal pleasanter for them as walks up Grisedale, ya kna, let aloan rights of foddering and goosage for freemen in Grasmere."

2. Toynbee, pp. 67 ff. Marx, Capital, p. 740.

3. Toynbee, p. 94.

difficult closing decade of the eighteenth century there appeared a number of important volumes bearing upon the condition of the agricultural
laborer, among them Thomas Ruggles' *History of the Poor* (1793–94.
2 vols.), David Davies' *The Case of the Labourers in Husbandry*
(1795), Frederic Eden's *The State of the Poor* (1797. 3 vols.). During
this period the laborer, as well as suffering from the agricultural revolution, was affected by a great rise in the price of grain, resulting variously
from population increase, the difficulty of importing grain in wartime,
and bad harvests. In 1800–1801, when wheat prices reached their peak,
England came nearer to famine than at any other time since the four-
teenth century.[4] When in May, 1800, Dorothy Wordsworth meets at
Rydal a woman begging who had never begged before, she comments,
". . . But these hard times!"[5] Clapham offers evidence to show that
the custom of great farmers dining with their laborers was being
abandoned about this time. He adds in parentheses: "You cease to feed
your men when it is hardest for them to feed themselves."[6]

There are some rather quaint suggestions issuing at this time from
conservative sources to explain the distress of the agricultural laborer.
That labor was improvident was the opinion of Sir Frederic Eden, in
his essay "On the Diet, Dress, Fuel, and Habitation, of the Labouring
Classes."[7] "There seems to be just reason to conclude that the miseries
of the labouring poor, arise less from the scantiness of their income,
(however much the philanthropist might wish it to be increased) than
from their own improvidence and unthriftiness . . ." The laborers in
the south of England, Eden found most extravagant. From week's end
to week's end they were indulging themselves in dry bread and cheese!
It was suggested by others that the English laborer eat mixed bread and
oatmeal, instead of his white loaf. But labor complained on the ground
that coarser breads acted as a laxative and made them unfit for hard
work![8] The Reverend David Davies, whose book the Hammonds tell
us made a profound impression on contemporary observers, denied the
charges of self-indulgence and sloth brought against the poor.[9] From
the latter charge Wordsworth was to defend the laborer in a poem
dated October 10, 1800.[1] On a September morning Coleridge, Dorothy,
and William were walking on the quiet eastern side of Grasmere, amusing themselves by observing what feathers, leaves, and twigs had been
washed ashore. As they idled along they heard the voices of busy reapers
in the field, women and men, boys and girls. Suddenly they saw on a
point extending into the lake the upright figure of a man, fishing! They
were immediately shocked to think that this peasant should be angling

4. *Idem*, p. 101.
6. Clapham, I, 122.
8. Hammond, pp. 99 ff.
9. See John Thelwall, *Tribune* (London, 1795–96. 2 vols.), Vol. II, No. 30, pp. 329 ff.
1. Wordsworth, *Poetical Works*, p. 148.

5. *Grasmere Journal*, May 14, 1800, in *Journals*.
7. *Annals*, xxviii (1797), 449–60.

when there were work and wages for labor in the fields. But as they approached him standing there alone by the calm lake, they noticed that he was worn by sickness, gaunt and lean, unable certainly to work in the fields.

> Too weak to labour in the harvest field,
> The Man was using his best skill to gain
> A pittance from the dead unfeeling lake
> That knew not of his wants.

Now there were many things for us, and the poet, to think of: the helplessness of the poor-sick in society, the virtue of the sick-poor who do what they can for their support and avoid seeking public relief, the habitual practice in the upper classes of misjudging the lower. Wordsworth named the point of land where the peasant was seen fishing "Rash Judgment."

Some improvers themselves recognized the injustice in the position of the laborer. Arthur Young modified his support of enclosure enough to wish to see some land held as a waste where the laborer might keep a pig.[2] "A man will love his country the better even for a pig." Sir John Sinclair, former president of the Board of Agriculture, accepted Young's idea; but not the board itself, which refused to let Young print this pamphlet under its name.[3] The earl of Winchelsea is conspicuous for showing a concern at this time for agricultural labor.[4] In an important essay "On Cottagers" appearing in the Georgical Essays (1803),[5] his lordship proposed that laborers be allowed to rent a small piece of land, an acre or two, and keep cows. On his own estate some seventy or eighty laborers were keeping one to four cows apiece. This same benevolent Lord Winchelsea, however, actually turned some of his tenants off their farms because they were related to the radical John Thelwall and read his publications.[6]

The case of Britton Abbot seemed to justify some concession to the country laborer. His story was told in the Annals of Agriculture in 1798;[7] in the Georgical Essays[8] the account was printed with comments by the editor, Dr. Hunter, who says: "This is the smiling picture of an industrious cottager and his family . . ." The story of Britton Abbot came originally from Thomas Bernard, Esq., who visited him at his cottage, two miles from Tadcaster on the road to York, in May, 1797. Abbot, now sixty-seven years old, had as a young man acquired a small farm, which he had given up to become a cottager, or laborer. An en-

2. Hammond, p. 60. 3. Ibid.
4. In his Memoir (p. 47) Bewick praised the late duke of Northumberland for having rented small portions of land reasonably to laborers, thinking thereby to raise their character as a class.
5. II (1803), 122–95. See also Annals, xxvi (1796), 227 ff.
6. Life of John Thelwall by His Widow (London, 1837), I, 144 n.
7. xxx (1798), 1–9. 8. II (1803), 305–31.

closure obliged him to quit his cottage, whereupon he applied to Squire
Fairfax for land on which to build a dwelling. This was granted: the
cottage was built, and Abbot worked as a day laborer, hoeing turnips,
at twelve to fifteen or eighteen shillings a week. Though he had had a
family of seven children, five of whom were living in 1797, he had never
been on relief. The moral of Britton Abbot's story is that the laborer,
even without his common rights, can with a very little help from the
landlords provide himself a decent, independent living. Help him with
his cottage and he will get along. Hunter's proposal is that cottages be
generally provided for laborers.

Picturesque cottages might be so disposed around a park, as to ornament and
enliven the scenery with much more effect, than *those misplaced Gothic
castles, and those pigmy models of Grecian temples,* that perverted taste is
so busy with: but it is the unfortunate principle of ornamental buildings in
England, that they should be *uninhabited* and *uninhabitable.*[9]

But if Hunter wants something done for the cottagers, he also wants
the cottagers to do much for themselves. He formulates for them golden
rules. Go to the cheapest market on Saturday, to church on Sunday, and
to labor on Monday.

   Hunter's taste for "picturesque cottages" reminds us that the cult of
the picturesque, which exhibited itself in painting, gardening, and
criticism, belonged to the late years of the eighteeenth century. Gilpin
was publishing his tours in search of picturesque landscape in the 1780's,
and a notable controversy over the picturesque "raged" in the last decade
of the century. In the work of Gilpin and Price one finds an agreement
on the common elements belonging to the picturesque. Both define it
as a wild beauty, marked by roughness, unevenness, and incivility. Gilpin
is inclined to identify the picturesque with Burke's "sublime," beauty
with terror in it—while Price establishes the picturesque as a category
midway between sublime and beautiful. Both definitions imply the wild,
if not the awesome.

   Accordingly, the lovers of the picturesque were no lovers of agriculture, which improved and civilized the natural landscape. Gilpin had
no relish for land which was merely fertile, calling such "a barren
prospect. I mean *barren* only in a picturesque light; for it affords good
pasturage; and is covered with herds of cattle; and a beautiful breed of
sheep . . ."[1] The cultivated scene "wears only a lovely smile."[2] The
improvements Gilpin saw on Mr. Graham's Netherby estate he spoke
of as having converted a waste into a thing "if not of beauty, at least of
fertility."[3] Such aesthetics just plow crops under. Archibald Alison says
in his *Essays on the Nature and Principles of Taste* (1790) : "The sub-

9. *Idem*, p. 319 n.   1. Gilpin, *Observations,* I, 35.
2. *Idem*, II, 7.   3. *Idem*, II, 127.

limest situations are often disfigured, by objects that we feel unworthy of them,—by the traces of cultivation, or attempts toward improvement . . ."[4] There was something nicely suicidal about the whole taste for the picturesque. It feasted on ruin. Gilpin thought that England with its "rich mutilation" of abbeys was more picturesque than still-Catholic France whose walls had not fallen to Protestant plunder. He spoke accordingly of Cromwell as having done more than any other Englishman to make his country picturesque![5]

It was somewhat ominous when the peasant cottage qualified for these impractical categories of the picturesque. This seems to have happened in the last decade of the eighteenth century. Uvedale Price, writing in 1794, approves the peasant cottage in picturesque landscape—with restrictions. It must not be painted white.

A cottage of quiet colour, half concealed among trees, with its bit of garden, its pales and orchard, is one of the most tranquil and soothing of all rural objects, and when the sun strikes upon it, and discovers a number of lively picturesque circumstances, one of the most chearful [sic] ; but if cleared round and whitened, its modest retired character is gone, and succeeded by a perpetual glare.

Sunshine, when it gilds some object of a sober tint, is like a smile that lights up a serious countenance ; a whitened object is like the eternal grin of a fool.[6]

The new vogue for picturesque cottages is reflected in the great number of architectural books on rural cottages which began to appear in the last decade of the eighteenth century.[7] Wordsworth was to show his distaste for this ironical fad in that nice poem describing his little summerhouse on the island of Grasmere,[8] a rustic lodge whose builder never saw the modern Morocco folios on rustic architecture with designs for

> . . . the rustic Lodge
> Antique, and Cottage with verandah graced,
> Nor lacking, for fit company, alcove,
> Green-house, shell-grot, and moss-lined hermitage.

4. (Dublin, 1790), p. 74.   5. Gilpin, *Observations*, II, 122.
6. *Essay on the Picturesque* (London, 1794), pp. 136-7. Wordsworth had the same aversion to white cottages. See *Guide through the District of the Lakes,* in *Prose Works*, II, 278. Dorothy was also opposed to white cottages and white churches. See *Early Letters*, pp. 427–8.
7. Charles Middleton, *Picturesque and Architectural Views for Cottages, Farm Houses, and Country Villas* (1791). John Soane, *Sketches in Architecture Containing Plans and Elevations of Cottages, Villas, and Other Useful Buildings . . .* (1793). James Malton, *An Essay on British Cottage Architecture* (1795). David Laing, *Hints for Dwellings; Consisting of Original Designs for Cottages, Farm-houses, Villas, &c. . . .* (1804). Robert Lugar, *Architectural Sketches for Cottages, Rural Dwellings, and Villas, in the Grecian, Gothic, and Fancy Styles . . .* (1805). Joseph Gandy, *Designs for Cottages, Cottage Farms, and Other Rural Buildings . . .* (1805). W. F. Pocock, *Architectural Designs for Rustic Cottages* (1807).
8. "Written with a Pencil upon a Stone in the Wall of the House (an Out-House), on the Island at Grasmere," in Wordsworth, *Poetical Works*, p. 547.

To his simple island shack Wordsworth would row, taking along fern
for his couch. There the sheep lay close around him,

> . . . nor, while from his bed
> He looks, through the open door-space, toward the lake
> And to the stirring breezes, does he want
> Creations lovely as the work of sleep—
> Fair sights, and visions of romantic joy!

5. *Poetic Economics*

The period of the agricultural revolution saw the creation of a great
body of literature and art devoted to the depiction and interpretation of
the peasant, and, as we might suppose, decay of peasant life was the
apparent theme in most of this work dealing with the rustic world, particularly that of the poets Goldsmith, Crabbe, Blake, Wordsworth, and
Clare. But there were exceptions, and notably the two famous Scottish
poems, Fergusson's "Farmer's Ingle," and Burns's "Cotter's Saturday
Night," neither of which seems to suggest a condition of distress. But
in Scotland one would have found circumstances very similar to those
in England, for here, to begin with, could be seen the same remarkable
improvement in agricultural methods. Sketching the social and economic
life of Scotland at the time of Burns's birth (1759), DeLancey Ferguson
properly pictures the rudeness of Scottish agriculture.[9] But improvements were under way, beginning, according to Hamilton, after the
Forty-five.[1] Kames started experimenting about 1747.[2] Scotland, we
are told, was first to adopt Tull's methods.[3] General improvement in
agriculture characterized the seventies.[4] The Lothians were the best-

9. J. DeLancey Ferguson, *Pride and Passion: Robert Burns, 1759–1796* (New York,
Oxford University Press, 1939), p. 10. See *Gent. Mag.,* xxiv (1754), 366–71, 416–22.
   1. Hamilton, p. 36.   2. *Idem,* p. 49.   3. Curtler, p. 178.
   4. Hamilton, p. 47. In John Galt's imaginary Dalmailing, Ayrshire, agricultural en-
terprise takes hold of the village in the year 1767. "All things in our parish were now

cultivated district in Great Britain by the close of the Napoleonic wars.[5] Sir John Sinclair, first president of the Board of Agriculture (1793), was of course a Scot.[6]

With the improvements went the familiar engrossing of the land, a process which proceeded more easily in Scotland than in England, for here the landlord's control over his land was very nearly absolute, there having developed in this country no order of yeomen comparable to that independent class below the Border. Scotland had been a much more feudal country and remained so until the last years of the eighteenth century, giving Walter Scott the privilege of seeing in the North the "sudden sunset" of the medieval world. This was a land of tenant farmers and laborers. And so in this period of agricultural improvement we see first in the region of the Scottish Highlands an easy and extensive displacement of tenants and laborers to make room for sheep. In the seventies emigration from this region was already tremendous.[7] Johnson, traveling here with Boswell in these years, was aware of the population shift and partially of its cause.[8] The exodus from the Highlands was in full swing in the 1790's.[9] Marx says that the dispossessed were at one time forbidden to emigrate to America and such regions in order to force them into the factories of Glasgow.[1] The same writer describes at length the later explusion of 15,000 people from the Sutherland estates between 1814 and 1820.[2] In the south of Scotland, where land was more profitably used for crops than for sheep-raising, we find the more familiar pattern, the development of large self-contained capitalistic farms in areas where small and open farming had been the rule.

While we think of Robert Fergusson as the vivid and realistic poet of the city, the poet of Auld Reikie—especially Edinburgh in the wintertime when the city had its full life—he did write one great rural poem, published in 1773, wherein he describes a country household with that same excellent realism employed in his city canvases. The tone of the "Farmer's Ingle" is one of dim cottage blackness, which the hearth hardly brightens. In the evening of a winter day a weary goodman returns to his cottage to eat with his family the good plain food beside a clean hearth, well stacked with sod and peat and turf. Aimless talk fol-

---

beginning to shoot up into a great prosperity. The spirit of farming began to get the upper hand of the spirit of smuggling . . ." *Annals of the Parish* (2d ed. Edinburgh, 1822), p. 83.

5. Hamilton, p. 56.   6. *DNB.*

7. Hamilton, pp. 69–70. See Margaret I. Adam, "The Causes of the Highland Emigrations of 1783–1803," *Scottish Historical Review,* XVII (1920), 78 ff.

8. Samuel Johnson, *Journey to the Western Islands of Scotland* [with Boswell's *Tour*], R. W. Chapman, ed. (London, Oxford University Press, 1924), pp. 33, 85–8, 90, 119–20.

9. Hamilton, p. 71.   1. Marx, *Capital,* p. 801.

2. *Idem,* pp. 801 ff.

lows their supper—of market, weather, church, marriages, bastards—
and then the children, not quarreling now since they have been fed,
listen awhile quietly to frightening stories of goblins and ghosts, equally
terrifying to the old.

> The mind's ay cradled whan the grave is near.

Dumbly the old people work on in the night with the spindle, making
yarn for clothing for the young. Lolling by the fire on the settle, the
goodman feeds the cat and collie bits of bread and cheese, while giving
small instructions for the morrow to his lads. And the goodwife too has
orders for her girls. Quietly the room grows dark and the household
sleepy.

> The cruizy too can only blink and bleer,
> The restit ingle's done the maist it dow . . .

And so sleep comes to farmer and cotter alike whose care serves all our
wants. In a great stanza, Fergusson has written one of the great poems
descriptive of country life, picturing its dull weariness and fatigue. But
this is a timeless rather than a timely poem: it is realistic in a larger
rather than a smaller way. While it describes a problem of rural life as
old as agriculture itself, the problem of toil and weariness, it suggests
in no way the immediate growing economic problems of the small-farmer
class.[3]

Similar omission characterizes Burns's "Cotter's Saturday Night,"
of the Kilmarnock volume of 1786, which professes to picture the household of a particular type of country laborer, a rather independent day
laborer, of the class described by Adam Smith in the following passage
in the *Wealth of Nations* (1776):

There still subsists in many parts of Scotland a set of people called Cotters or
Cottagers, though they were more frequent some years ago than they are now.
They are a sort of out-servants of the landlords and farmers. The usual re-
ward which they receive from their masters is a house, a small garden for
pot-herbs, as much grass as will feed a cow, and, perhaps, an acre or two of
bad arable land. When their master has occasion for their labour, he gives
them, besides, two pecks of oatmeal a week, worth about sixteenpence ster-
ling. During a great part of the year he had little or no occasion for their labour, and the cultivation of their own little possession is not sufficient to
occupy the time which is left at their own disposal. When such occupiers were

3. Fergusson may have had knowledge of one side of the agricultural revolution. At
the University of St. Andrews he formed a friendship with Professor Wilkie and
visited his farm four miles from the city. *The Poetical Works of Robert Fergusson* . . .
A. B. Grosart, ed. (London, 1878), p. li. Wilkie was a professor of natural history and
a progressive farmer who experimented in the new ways of agriculture. He fertilized his
acres with the street manure of St. Andrews, not previously used for farm purposes. See
note prefatory to Fergusson's "Eclogue to the Memory of Dr. William Wilkie" (*idem*,
pp. 29-30).

more numerous than they are at present, they are said to have been willing to give their spare time for a very small recompense to anybody, and to have wrought for less wages than other labourers.[4]

The cotter class, this passage definitely indicates, was disappearing in 1776, but Burns's poem published ten years later hardly intimates economic plight. He does perhaps suggest that the cotter is threatened, but the dangers are social rather than economic: he fears the extension into the country of luxury, and by luxury he means simply the social vices. Not in this famous poem, but in lesser pieces in the same volume, Burns has told of the suffering of the small tenants on the land and perhaps pointed rightly to the cause. His mousie and his mountain daisy, we note, both come to grief at the stroke of the plow, the one losing its field home, the other its very life in the furrow. Are not these two poems in a way most proper and successful symbols of the agricultural revolution?[5]

Two notable prose writings dealing at a somewhat later date with the village likewise ignored features of decay that must have been all too apparent. We refer to Washington Irving's *Sketch Book* (1819–20) and Miss Mitford's *Our Village* (1824–32). By the time Irving was doing his English sketching, the depression following the Napoleonic wars had added to the extreme hardship of the rural world. But the romantic Irving skipped over the economic fact of the countryside to write of English rural society as though it were still one happy family of benevolent landowners, substantial yeomen, and contented laborers. Fact enters his record only to be hidden. Speaking of the independence belonging to all country classes, he says:

This, it must be confessed, is not so universally the case at present as it was formerly; the larger estates having, in late years of distress, absorbed the smaller; and, in some parts of the country, almost annihilated the sturdy race of small farmers. These, however, I believe, are but casual breaks in the general system I have mentioned.[6]

Miss Mitford's pre-Victorian pages of *Our Village* reveal a similar determination to charm the "gentle reader," no matter what falsification

4. *Wealth of Nations,* I, 122.
5. There are a few biographical facts relating Burns to the agricultural revolution. As a laborer on his father's farm he read Tull and Dickson on agriculture. See J. Currie, *Life of Robert Burns,* in *The Works of Robert Burns,* J. Currie, ed. (2d ed. London, 1801. 4 vols.), I, 43. He was said to have prided himself on the straightness of his furrows. When he was in Edinburgh, Mrs. Dunlop, who was concerned for his future, suggested that he apply for the then discussed chair of agriculture in Edinburgh University. *Cambridge History of English Literature,* XI, 245. On his tour of Scotland in 1787, Burns was a guest at a farmers' club at Kelso on May 14: "—all gentlemen talking of high matters—each of them keeps a hunter from 30£. to 50£. value, and attends the fox-hunting club in the country." Currie, *Life of Robert Burns,* in *The Works of Robert Burns,* I, 160–1.
6. *The Sketch Book* (World's Classics ed. London, Oxford University Press, 1921), p. 80.

is necessary. The gentle reader is of course hurried past the poorhouse with the author's assurance that the inmates are likely much better off than we suppose or imagine.[7] We meet prosperous yeomen in this village, such as Farmer Allen, who owns what in Berkshire is called "a little bargain," a farm of 30 or 40 acres, which he cultivates with the help of his son. His family lives very comfortably, the produce of the land being supplemented by the dairy, poultry yard, and orchard. With not enough emphasis Miss Mitford says that the Allens belong to "an order of cultivators now passing rapidly away, but in which much of the best part of the English character, its industry, its frugality, its sound sense, and its kindness might be found."[8]

Not in all work dealing with the peasant, but in most of it, there is apt recognition of the declining condition of the smaller classes in the country, though, as we shall see, this recognition is not always accompanied by a just understanding of the extent to which the forces of the agricultural revolution were responsible for the hardship of the peasantry.

Goldsmith's *Deserted Village,* published in 1770, took as its theme the very subject of the depopulation of the English village. Macaulay said Goldsmith's village was an impossible fiction, that the smiling prosperous village of the poem belonged to England, while the village in ruin was Goldsmith's recollection of his native impoverished Ireland.[9] But this historian's opinion seems generally to have been discredited. Paul Mantoux, in his history of the industrial revolution in eighteenth-century England, quotes Goldsmith's poem as authentic description of the time,[1] and R. S. Crane supports the opinion, "even yet slightly heretical, that the immediate social background . . . [of the *Deserted Village*] must be sought in England . . ."[2] Lecky would seem to disavow Macaulay's criticism, for he quotes from Goldsmith's poem.[3] A reviewer of the *Deserted Village* in the *Gentleman's Magazine* in the year the poem appeared, we might add, remarks that while Goldsmith was certainly unrealistic in picturing the village in prosperity, he need not have drawn upon his imagination in describing the deserted village[4] —a nice reversal of Macaulay!

For the "thinning" of "mankind" evident in the land Goldsmith blamed that old eighteenth-century gentleman Luxury, who almost becomes personified in his poem in a flushed and florid social wreck. The *Deserted Village* was, then, a late rebuttal of the optimistic philosophy of Bernard Mandeville's *Fable of the Bees* (1714), which said that

7. Mary Russell Mitford, *Our Village,* A. T. Ritchie, ed., illustrated by Hugh Thomson (London, Macmillan, 1893), pp. 61-4.
8. *Idem,* p. 115.
9. Lord Macaulay, "Oliver Goldsmith," *Encyclopaedia Britannica* (11th ed.).
1. Mantoux, p. 181.
2. R. S. Crane, *New Essays by Oliver Goldsmith* (Chicago, University of Chicago Press, 1927), Introduction, p. xl.
3. Lecky, VI, 198, n. 2.   4. *Gent. Mag.,* XL (1770), 271.

private vices create public benefits, that selfish spending and luxurious living create paradoxically a social good in the form of great industrial activity in the human hive. Goldsmith would show that out of evil comes not good but, what one might expect, more evil. In this instance the evil is the destruction of England's bold peasantry. In his fear of luxury the Irish Goldsmith showed, perhaps, the uneasiness of a son of a simpler and poorer civilization when confronted with the richer life of England. Opposition to luxury had a tradition in poor Ireland. Bishop Berkeley, classmate in Dublin of Goldsmith's favorite uncle Contarini, was a major opponent of Mandeville,[5] and Francis Hutcheson, another critic of the *Fable of the Bees,* was writing in Dublin.[6]

The particular luxury Goldsmith points to in his poem is that which permits a rich nabob to buy up a village like Auburn as land for a private park and pleasure ground.[7] The cottages are pulled down, and it is only by the flowers, now going wild, that the poet is able to locate the vanished dwellings. In the case of Auburn the purchaser seems to have done nothing very formal, for the streams are now stopped with sedge, and long grass overgrows the moldering wall. A similar conversion of a village Goldsmith had considered much earlier, in an essay entitled "The Revolution in Low Life," recently assigned to him by Mr. Crane in *New Essays by Oliver Goldsmith* (1927). Here he had described a visit made during the summer of 1761 to an English village some fifty miles from London, a sweet village of near a hundred houses, which were about to be emptied and destroyed to make room for the estate of a London merchant who was going to turn the whole thing into a pleasure seat.

Goldsmith's understanding of depopulation was more complex, however, than our remarks suggest. To the word "luxury" as used in this poem Goldsmith, ambiguously, gave a second meaning—a meaning which the age must have rather generally extended to the term. In this second sense luxury means trade and industry, and thus Goldsmith was attacking the manufacturing and commerce that were unsettling England's basic rural economy. Goldsmith was enough of a physiocrat to feel that a country whose economy was not fundamentally agricultural was terribly exposed to the winds.

> Teach erring man to spurn the rage of gain :
> Teach him, that states of native strength possest,
> Though very poor, may still be very blest ;
> That trade's proud empire hastes to swift decay,

5. See *Alciphron, or the Minute Philosopher* (London, 1732), Second Dialogue; also Mandeville's reply to Berkeley, *Letter to Dion* (1732).

6. Francis Hutcheson, *Inquiry into the Original of Our Ideas of Beauty and Virtue* (London, 1725) ; *Observations on the Fable of the Bees,* in *Hibernicus Letters* (Dublin), February 4, 12, 19, 1726. See Adam Smith, *Wealth of Nations,* E. Cannan, ed. (New York, Modern Library, 1937), p. xlviii.

7. For the use of villages for parks, see Gray, p. 121.

As ocean sweeps the laboured mole away;
While self-dependent power can time defy,
As rocks resist the billows and the sky.

The merchants and manufacturers were Goldsmith's devils for two rea-
sons—first, for their careless self-indulgence which would use a village
for a park, and secondly, in a much graver way, for developing an in-
secure commercial and industrial nation.[8]

The commercial classes, Goldsmith made more directly responsible
for the depopulation of the land than they actually were. Their direct
injury to English villages was generally limited to the metropolitan
area of London which may have been the locale of the excursions Goldsmith refers to in the Dedication of his poem.[9] The real immediate de-
populators were of course the landowners and great farmers, whose
activities affected the entire farming world of England. And the conservative Goldsmith in his timely poem quite overlooked the guilt of
these landed groups. This omission is the more surprising in view of
another essay ascribed by Mr. Crane to Goldsmith, on "The Progress
of the Arts in Switzerland: the New Agricultural Society at Berne"
(*Public Ledger,* August 29, 1761). This essay shows an early-bird
awareness of the agricultural revolution, which was responsible among
other things for this early agricultural society. The writer of this essay
has the first volume of the society's publications in his hand (*Recueil de
memoires* . . . , 1760). In the first part of the article he speaks of agriculture as one of "the arts of population," saying the Swiss realize this
and are beginning accordingly to cultivate their mountains. The writer
quotes testimony from the *Recueil* to the pre-eminence of English ways
of farming and then proceeds to criticize the peasant for being unprogressive. The essay ends on a low note, with instructions for the grafting of
walnut trees and a cure for the bite of a mad dog. If this is Goldsmith's
essay, we must believe that he had some awareness of the agricultural
revolution which was more directly harmful to the English village than
the commerce and industry he solely condemns. The omission in the
Deserted Village of the major role the landed class had in this social
change prevents the poem from making economic sense about a condition to which Goldsmith was very properly attentive.

Crabbe's *Village* (1783), a study in the lives of country laborers, appearing some years after Goldsmith's poem, describes not one village
but two—one where the soil is sandy and barren, a bleak seacoast village, and a second in a more fertile part of England. Both are unlovely.
In the lean village of charlock and mallow fields we find a savage, surly

8. Howard J. Bell, in his article *"The Deserted Village* and Goldsmith's Social Doctrines," argues that Goldsmith is thinking more of England's commercial development
than of her somewhat less apparent industrial development. *Publications of the Modern
Language Association,* LIX (1944), 748–9.
9. But see above, p. 31, n. 7, and below, p. 42.

people, unable and unwilling to labor on the hard soil. Instead, they play the good old eighteenth-century games of smuggling and decoying ships to the shore for plunder at night.

> Here, wand'ring long, amid these frowning fields,
> I sought the simple life that Nature yields;
> Rapine and Wrong and Fear usurp'd her place,
> And a bold, artful, surly, savage race . . .

From this scene we turn to the other village of fertile fields, and here Crabbe singles out for description a virtuous laborer who has always done his best.

> He once was chief in all the rustic trade;
> His steady hand the straightest furrow made;
> Full many a prize he won, and still is proud
> To find the triumphs of his youth allow'd . . .

When old age comes upon this fine rustic, he is obliged to labor for one man and another, all of whom are dissatisfied and label him "lazy poor." Since his own children also lack mercy, there is nothing left for him but the poorhouse,

> Whose walls of mud scarce bear the broken door;
>
> .   .   .   .
>
> There children dwell who know no parents' care;
> Parents, who know no children's love, dwell there!

Here in a room of mud and lath and thatch, lighted through one dull pane, the shattered man lies ill on a dusty matted flock. (Crabbe is never so fine as when he is describing anything medical.) A quack doctor paid by the town visits the poorhouse,

> With speed that, entering, speaks his haste to go.

Equally brief is the call of the parish priest—not a pious man, rich on forty pounds a year, but a jovial youth, who gives his mornings to hunting and his evenings to feasting and love-making.

> Shall he sit sadly by the sick man's bed,
> To raise the hope he feels not, or with zeal
> To combat fears that e'en the pious feel?

Death comes at last for the man of many sorrows.

> Now to the church behold the mourners come,
> Sedately torpid and devoutly dumb . . .

Only the village children feel the loss.

> For he was one in all their idle sport,
> And like a monarch ruled their little court.

The pliant bow he form'd, the flying ball,
The bat, the wicket, were his labours all;
Him now they follow to his grave, and stand
Silent and sad, and gazing, hand in hand . . .

The priest was too busy to come immediately for the service, so the
body lay many days unburied. Here is a final image of the socio-medical
contamination Crabbe would have us sense.

In Crabbe's villages we see economic hardship and its effects on the
life of the laborers, making the good man suffer and corrupting others
into thievery and vice. While we recognize in these ironical couplets a
spirit of indignation proper in the poetry of a young man whose own
youth had been hard, it is noteworthy that Crabbe does not point to
any one economic fact, such as enclosure, as central in the disturbance
of village manners. Many years later, in 1807, he resumed his village
material in the *Parish Register*. Not a struggling young medico now,
but a clergyman enjoying distinguished conservative patronage, Crabbe
has come to adopt a pietistic attitude toward the rural misery he sees
(and he sees much less now than he did before the French Revolution).
If people are destitute, it is because they are wicked. In the Preface
Crabbe tells us that this later work is "an endeavour once more to describe village-manners, not by adopting the notion of pastoral simplicity
or assuming ideas of rustic barbarity, but by more natural views of the
peasantry, considered as a mixed body of persons, sober or profligate,
and hence, in a great measure, contented or miserable."[1] And so in the
Parish Register we see both idyllic and wretched peasant homes, the circumstances varying with the character of the people. The virtuous live
in vine-covered sun-bathed cottages, with copies of Bunyan and the
Bible on the table, and on the walls pictures of Louis, Charles, Godiva.
Sunday evening after service these innocents sit in pretty flower gardens
mid carnations, pinks, and tulips.[2] But in the homes where there is drinking and card-playing and poaching equipment, we find squalor and
misery.[3] Here children sleep in the same beds with their parents and are
there first introduced to facts of life. That the condition of a peasantry
depends upon its character is now the moral judgment of the minister-
poet Crabbe, who had meanwhile been thirteen years an absentee from
his own country parish of Muston.

The poet Cowper has a certain affinity with the later Crabbe in judging
the conditions he saw among the English peasantry, with whom, however, his rural poetry is not greatly concerned. As a rural poet, Cowper
tells us chiefly about his own convalescent life in the country where, under
the supervision of the nature-minded physician Heberden, he was at-

1. *The Poetical Works of George Crabbe*, A. J. Carlyle and R. M. Carlyle, eds. (London, Oxford University Press, 1914), p. 23.
2. *Idem*, pp. 51–2.   3. *Idem*, pp. 52–3.

tempting to recover and keep his balance of mind. In the *Task* (1785), which describes this sojourn in the lands across from Judea, we see a patient-poet stretching his legs on an afternoon walk or retreating slightly fagged into the shade of a colonnade; or we find him in his garden trying to raise a superior cucumber. Again we see him of a winter evening on a sofa by the fireside, sipping the cup that cheers but does not inebriate. Cowper was a poet of cozy domestic life in the country. But his own snug winter evenings sometimes made him think, by contrast, of a poor cottage family, with only twigs on their hearth for warmth, with but a poor taper for light, with brown bread for their evening meal, without sauce, butter, or cheese.[4] But though he pities the peasant's suffering, he is slow to sense economic injustice. Cowper was never such a Horatian that he could leave behind his box of sermons when he turned to the country. He must continue his pious preaching and scolding, and accordingly he declares that peasant misery is

> Th' effect of laziness or sottish waste.[5]

The pub is the curse of the country and one of the chief causes of its distress.

> Pass where we may, through city or through town,
> Village, or hamlet, of this merry land,
> Though lean and beggar'd, ev'ry twentieth pace
> Conducts th' unguarded nose to such a whiff
> Of stale debauch, forth-issuing from the styes
> That law has licens'd, as makes temp'rance reel.
> There sit, involv'd and lost in curling clouds
> Of Indian fume, and guzzling deep, the boor,
> The lackey, and the groom: the craftsman there
> Takes a Lethean leave of all his toil;
> Smith, cobbler, joiner, he that plies the shears,
> And he that kneads the dough; all loud alike,
> All learned, and all drunk![6]

The indulgences of the village are a replica of the luxury of the city. Innocence, he finds, is so completely absent from the country as to make the pastoral dream an impossibility, as it had not been for Sidney or Maro. The rural lass wears lappets "aloft," ribbons streaming away, high French heels.

> The town has ting'd the country; and the stain
> Appears a spot upon a vestal's robe,
> The worse for what it soils.[7]

Amid his moralizing about country manners, Cowper does mention one political evil, "universal soldiership,"[8] which sends the country fel-

4. *Task*, Bk. IV, ll. 374 ff.
6. *Idem*, Bk. IV, ll. 466 ff.
8. *Idem*, Bk. IV, l. 617.

5. *Idem*, Bk, IV, l. 431.
7. *Idem*, Bk. IV, ll. 553 ff.

lows back to the land debased by their three years in the service. Otherwise he seems not to be appreciative or aware of the social forces co-
operating to corrupt peasant life. This is surprising in the light of the
fact that Cowper elsewhere shows economic understanding and vision.
He is, for instance, able to conceive of a world without trade barriers, in
which man is being both properly fed and civilized by the intercourse of
nations.

> . . . the band of commerce was design'd
> T' associate all the branches of mankind;
> And, if a boundless plenty be the robe,
> Trade is the golden girdle of the globe.
> Wise to promote whatever end he means,
> God opens fruitful nature's various scenes:
> Each climate needs what other climes produce,
> And offers something to the gen'ral use;
> No land but listens to the common call,
> And in return receives supply from all.[9]

Vision in the direction of world economy seems to have been accompanied in Cowper's case by an almost total blindness to the realities of the
economy of his beloved rural scene. He is, in fact, less satisfactory in
treating the immediate economic scene than is a poet like Blake, whom
we might expect to find writing quite without place or bound.

Blake's *Songs of Innocence and Experience* (1789, 1793), unlike
much of his later poetry, are firmly set in the late eighteenth-century
scene. They employ its new ballad measures, in a most lyrical form;
they reflect ethical theories developed by moralists of the age; and
furthermore they deal, in part at least, with the decay of peasant life in
that English countryside which had been an early love of this London-
born poet. In a Carlylean biography of this Diogenes, Gilchrist says of
Blake, "As he grew older the lad became fond of roving out into the
country, a fondness in keeping with the romantic turn."[1] A favorite
day's walk in later years was to Blackheath, over the Dulwich and Nor-
wood hills, to Croydon, and on to Walton-upon-Thames.[2] He liked best
the country to the south of London—Surrey, Sussex, and Kent, "with
their delightful mixture of arable, pasture, woodland, waste, and down
. . ."[3] Blake's first vision as a lad came, significantly, in the country:
on Peckham Rye, by Dulwich Hill, he saw a tree full of angels![4]

In introducing the *Songs of Innocence* Blake had very properly written:

---

9. "Charity," ll. 83 ff.
1. Alexander Gilchrist, *Life of William Blake* (London, John Lane, 1928), p. 6.
2. *Idem,* p. 7.   3. *Idem,* p. 372.
4. *Idem,* p. 7.

And I made a rural pen,
And I stain'd the water clear,
And I wrote my happy songs
Every child may joy to hear.

These songs picture the happy life of the child on the village green, common, and farm—in a blessed world of lamb-like innocence, to which the
little sweeps return when freed from their coffins by Blake's ever-present
angels. The child's expulsion from this pastoral Eden is partly the
subject of the later bitter volume, the *Songs of Experience*.

Because I was happy upon the heath,
And smil'd among the winter's snow,
They clothed me in the clothes of death,
And taught me to sing the notes of woe.[5]

The child as symbol of man has been transplanted to a London of crying
infants and cursing harlots and sighing soldiers: the child as child has
gone, in these early days of child labor, into the service of factories and
chimneys—chimneys that were becoming increasingly sooty with the
use of coal. We would not, of course, nor could we, limit the meaning
of these *Songs*. They speak of more than economic oppression: they
tell, in fact, the whole story of the imprisonment of man within the chains
of society, particularly the confinement of his passion. But we cannot
avoid reading into these *Songs* the same story of the English countryside which was being told by all poets. The young Blake was not indif-
ferent to economic matters. It is interesting to note that in his early
historical drama, *King Edward the Third*, published in 1783, he had
introduced for discussion the modern physiocratic hypothesis that a nation's wealth is founded in its agriculture.[6] But it is not made clear in
Blake's *Songs* precisely what forms of evil and self-interest have caused
the destruction of rural life. One would infer, I think, that these forces
were industrial and urban rather than agrarian. Blake's "Tyger," burning bright in the forest of the night, with its orange stripes flaming
against blackness, might easily appear to our imaginations as a great
modern blast furnace. Significantly, the imagery Blake has chosen for
handling his tiger is that of the forge—fire, chains, anvils, tongs, ham-
mer. The symbolism we suggest for this key poem of the *Songs of Experience* is borne out by the picture Blake gives us of modern London
in his later *Jerusalem*. It is a city of furnaces and heavy hammers and
anvils of death. It is a city, too, of factories and industrial wheels-

---

5. "The Chimney Sweeper," *Poetry and Prose of William Blake*, Geoffrey Keynes, ed.
(London, Nonesuch Press, 1939), p. 70.
6.   Say, Lords, should not our thoughts be first to commerce?
        My Lord Bishop, you would recommend us agriculture?
                        Poetry and Prose of William Blake, p. 23.

without-wheels—Blake himself preferring wheels-within-wheels. It is the city of Locke and Newton, where the "Loom of Locke" is turned by the "Water-wheels of Newton." Everything suggests that in so far as he dealt with economic matters Blake directed moral censure chiefly against industrial and urban powers. In neglecting at the same time the part agrarian forces had in the ruin of innocence, he reflected the prevailing thought habits of his time, shared, among others, by Wordsworth.

Wordsworth is reported to have said that, "although he was known to the world only as a poet, he had given twelve hours' thought to the condition and prospects of society for one to poetry."[7] The full pattern of Wordsworth's agrarian thought in reference to the economic scene is examined in the last of these essays. We shall speak here only of his relations to the agricultural revolution. It is abundantly clear, from quotations already made from his writings, that he was familiar with the main features of the agricultural revolution—its cattle breeding, its improving bishops, and also its enclosure. In *Guilt and Sorrow* (1794), we may note, he used as the scene of his social tragedy the empty countryside of Salisbury plain, with its long yellow fields of corn. Here the sailor is searching for some sign of human life, a small cottage that would be hospitable, but there is no humble life on these plains. There is no gipsy over his fire of furze, or laborer by his red kiln; no taper glimmers from the sick man's room; no lamp shines from the tollgate house. The search for a place to hide his head brings the sailor to a spital, built in Christian times as a shelter for the shepherd but now a ruin, on account, I suppose, of these wastes of grain. This landscape is definitely improved England. Tom Poole, who was identified with the yeoman in Wordsworth's mind, wrote in October of 1800 a series of papers on "Monopolists and Farmers," which Coleridge published, with some alterations, in the *Morning Post*.[8] Wordsworth must have been familiar with their content and general ideas. But it so happened that his own Lake country was not conspicuously affected by the agricultural revolution and the enclosure movement until a period much later than the *Preface* of 1800 and its related poems. The economic experience of the Lake counties, whose peasantry chiefly concerned Wordsworth, was hardly typical, for here, as we shall see, the forces hostile to the peasant were principally industrial. Accordingly, the main charge of Wordsworth's economic criticism was directed at the new factory system rather than at the new developments in agriculture.

This indeed seems to be a pattern in these times, to neglect the part the landlords and improvers had in creating distress in the country. The explanation for this pleasant courtesy is probably to be found in

---

7. A remark made to the Reverend Orville Dewey. See Harper, pp. 596-7.
8. See article on Poole in *DNB*.

a conservative allegiance to the landed interests in England. But there were some well-informed writers and artists who were properly critical of the agricultural revolution, among them Thomas Bewick, the wood engraver, whose talent Wordsworth envied.

O now that the genius of Bewick were mine,
And the skill which he learned on the banks of the Tyne,
Then the Muses might deal with me just as they chose,
For I'd take my last leave both of verse and of prose.[9]

Bewick was born in 1753 in Northumberland, at Cherry-burn House, situated on the south side of the Tyne River. His childhood was not unlike Wordsworth's, and it begot the man. As one reads his *Memoir*, written between 1822 and 1828, one thinks often of the *Prelude*. Like Wordsworth, he listened with delight to the murmuring hum which flowed by his father's house.[1] Those who have been brought up in the country, he says, receive therefrom a lifelong flow of animal spirits "such as very few, or none, brought up in a town ever know . . ."[2] The country was the inspiration and the object of his art, which expressed itself first in paintings of hunting scenes for the cottage walls of his rustic Northumbrian neighbors.[3] He left Cherry-burn as a boy to become apprenticed to a Newcastle engraver but returned in 1774 to spend two pleasurable years back in the country. In 1776 he went to London but could not abide the great city. He at least would live by the Tyneside, and next year he returned to Newcastle where he did his life's work.

Looking back over the years in his *Memoir* Bewick is bitter about the forces of improvement and enclosure which in his own life span had destroyed English rural life. In 1774 the Cherry-burn region was still unchanged.

About Christmas, as I had done before when a boy, I went with my father to a distance to collect the money due to him for coals. In these rounds, I had

9. "The Two Thieves," ll. 1–4, Wordsworth, *Poetical Works*, p. 571.
1. *Memoir*, p. 11.   2. *Idem*, p. 217.   3. *Idem*, p. 7.

the opportunity of witnessing the kindness and hospitality of the people. The countenances of all, both high and low, beamed with cheerfulness; and this was heightened everywhere by the music of old tunes, from the well-known, exhilarating, wild notes of the Northumberland pipes, amidst the buzz occasioned by "foulpleughs" (morrice or sword dancers) from various parts of the country. This altogether left an impression on my mind which the cares of the world have never effaced from it. The gentry, the farmers, and even the working people, of that day had their Christmas home-brewed ale, made only from malt and hops. This was before the pernicious use of chemical compounds was known, or agricultural improvements had quickened the eyes of landlords, banished many small farmers, soured their countenances, and altered for the worse the characters of the larger ones that remained.[4]

About this time (1776) Bewick took a walking trip through Cumberland, and then north to the Highlands of Scotland, avoiding towns and inns.[5] He was entertained at farmhouses by a people whom he describes as unpolluted, unspoiled, honorable, kind. "From that time to this, I have ever felt pleased at the name of Highlander."

Is it not to be regretted that agricultural improvements have taught the landlords, or chieftains, to turn numerous farms into one, and to banish thousands of these hardy descendants of the ancient Britons,—these brave race of men to whose forefathers they owed so much,—to seek an asylum in foreign climes? In exchange for *men*, they have filled the country with sheep![6]

It was in 1812 that the common near Cherry-burn, containing 1,852 acres, was divided. The division, Bewick says, gave the land to those who already had too much—rich farmers and landlords—and took it away from the poor—the laborers and small farmers.[7] Bewick was especially fond of the laborer who got much of his living from this waste.

To the westward, adjoining the house, lay the common or fell, which extended some few miles in length, and was of various breadths. It was mostly fine, green sward or pasturage, broken or divided, indeed, with clumps of "blossom'd whins," foxglove, fern, and some junipers, and with heather in profusion, sufficient to scent the whole air. Near the burns, which guttered its sides, were to be seen the remains of old oaks, hollowed out by Time, with alders, willows, and birch, which were often to be met with in the same state; and these seemed to me to point out the length of time that these domains had belonged to no one. On this common,—the poor man's heritage for ages past, where he kept a few sheep, or a Kyloe cow, perhaps a flock of geese, and mostly a stock of bee-hives,—it was with infinite pleasure that I long beheld the beautiful wild scenery which was there exhibited, and it is with the opposite feelings of regret that I now find all swept away. Here and there on this common were to be seen the cottage, or rather hovel, of some labouring man, built at his own expense, and mostly with his own hands; and to this he always added a garth and a garden, upon which great pains and labour

4. *Idem,* pp. 80-1.   5. *Idem,* pp. 82 ff.
6. *Idem,* p. 90.   7. *Idem,* p. 34 n.

were bestowed to make both productive; and for this purpose not a bit of manure was suffered to be wasted away on the "lonnings" or public roads. These various concerns excited the attention and industry of the hardy occupants, which enabled them to prosper, and made them despise being ever numbered with the parish poor. These men, whose children were neither pampered nor spoiled, might truly be called—

"A bold peasantry, their country's pride;"

and to this day I think I see their broad shoulders and their hardy sun-burnt looks, which altogether bespoke the vigour of their constitutions.

These cottagers (at least those of them I knew) were of an honest and independent character, while at the same time they held the neighbouring gentry in the greatest estimation and respect; and these, again, in return, did not over-look them, but were interested in knowing that they were happy and well. Most of these poor men, from their having little intercourse with the world, were in all their actions and behaviour truly original; and, except reading the Bible, local histories, and old ballads, their knowledge was generally limited.[8]

There follows in the *Memoir* a descriptive catalogue of several of these cottagers—laborers, not farmers—who lived on this common beside Cherry-burn. There is Will Bewick, who first gave the artist a "general knowledge of astronomy and of the magnitude of the universe."[9] Another dweller on the common was Anthony Liddell,[1] one whom Bewick calls a sort of village Hampden, one who was perfectly read in the Bible, where he learned the illegal truth that the birds of the air and the fish of the sea were made by God for the enjoyment of all men. With this authority he boldly disregarded the game laws and shot continually, if not accurately, except when his gun rested on a hayfork. He was repeatedly brought before the justices of the peace; he always pleaded his own case; the justices were always amused; and Liddell always went to gaol, where he reread his Bible. His other reading consisted of Josephus, the *Holy Wars,* and Bishop Taylor's *Sermons.* His clothes were, like the country dress Addison describes, of an old fashion, dating back many reigns. Third in Bewick's catalogue is Thomas Foster,[2] who kept sheep on the fells but was rather more interested in his bees. He had beehives all over the common, hidden in secret spots among whin bushes. The busy bees eventually made this frugal and industrious man relatively rich. The longest account perhaps is that of John Chapman,[3] who worked for Bewick's father. Chapman lived closely enough on bread, potatoes, and oatmeal but every so often posted off to Newcastle for a few days of beer. These trips had the purpose of "lowsening his skin." He was a great character to the tradesmen of Newcastle, who spoiled him a bit.

8. *Idem,* pp. 33–5.
1. *Idem,* pp. 36–8.
3. *Idem,* pp. 40–2.

9. *Idem,* p. 35.
2. *Idem,* pp. 38–9.

In reflecting upon such cottagers Bewick says that he thinks these inhabitants of the wastes and fells enjoyed health and happiness in a degree surpassing most men. Their food was simple, consisting on weekdays of bread, oatmeal, milk; on Sundays, of a little meat and cabbage. Bewick thought that as a class the poor laboring men were more intelligent than the farmers. They read more, thought more, had a keener ear for news. The farmers, "being more exclusively occupied with the management of their farms, . . . read but little."[4]

Another person who was well aware of what was happening on the land in these days was John Thelwall, London-born friend of Coleridge and Wordsworth, who contributed to the drama of a revolutionary period. Trained like Danton to be an advocate, Thelwall entered politics via Coachmakers' Hall and was active in the political life of England for seven or eight years, until his retirement to the country in 1797. He had become notorious for his participation in the activities of the political societies of leftwing tendencies in the 1790's.[5]

Thelwall's radicalism was partly encouraged by his firsthand understanding of the conditions prevailing in the English farming world. He had always liked to walk in the country, perhaps because of the benefit to his health. On an excursion in the summer of 1789 this son of a London mercer met his wife down in Rutlandshire.

The comparison between the town-bred fiction of fashionable life, and the innocent reality of rustic purity, operated in favour of the modest country-girl, and the romantic idea entered his head that he might develop the germs of intellect which were so inherent in this child of nature, and like Mr. Day, the author of "Sanford and Merton," educate his future wife.[6]

On his country rambles Thelwall was able to observe the changes in agriculture he was to complain of, particularly in the issues of the *Tribune* published in 1795. Everywhere in England he saw land monopoly. In parishes where there were formerly nine, twelve, fifteen farms, you now had at most five, six, or seven.[7] "Cannibal farmers," Thelwall calls these engrossers of the land. In certain areas cottages were falling before that even less wholesome taste for parks and pleasure grounds described earlier by Goldsmith.[8] In the sixteenth *Tribune* lecture, Thelwall, recently returned from a walk down in Surrey, refers to this county as the "Gentleman's County," "because, forsooth the beggarly *sans*

---

4. *Idem*, p. 46.
5. See *Life of John Thelwall by His Widow*, chap. v, and following.
6. *Idem*, p. 38.   7. *Tribune*, Vol. ii, No. 32, p. 376.
8. In a letter on gardening addressed from Grasmere to Sir George Beaumont ,(October 17, 1805), Wordsworth complained that great mansions, like the upas tree, were breathing out death and desolation by expelling villages of human creatures from their neighborhood. The expulsion of humankind from the landscape meant, he said, a falsification of nature, and furthermore removed the best audience for the art of landscape gardening to address itself to. *Early Letters*, pp. 527–8.

culottes are routed out from it; their vulgar cottages, so offensive to the proud eye of luxury, are exterminated, and nothing but the stately domes of useless grandeur present themselves to our eyes."[9] Down on the Isle of Wight he saw the same thing, mansions of luxury rising, farms turned into summer estates and *fermes ornées* for the wealthy.[1]

Big farms, cottages disappearing, and a people emigrating from England! Thelwall's first lecture for the *Tribune* deals with this problem of the "depopulation" of England. In this essay he repeats in his own way the familiar lines from the *Deserted Village:*

> Princes and Lords may flourish, and may fade;
> A breath may make them, as a breath hath made;
> But a bold Peasantry, their Country's pride!
> When once 'tis lost, can never be supplied.

Thelwall often mentions the fact that in the summer of 1794 alone upwards of 80,000 emigrated to the United States from the British Isles. The fine yeomen are leaving England, and on the land remains a poor population of laborers whose condition is wretched. These laborers Thelwall was seeing in his excursions about England, for it was his habit to drop into the little hedge alehouses and sit down with the rough clowns in their tattered garments. In behalf of labor Thelwall undertook to popularize in the pages of his *Tribune* the findings in the Reverend David Davies' pamphlet, *The Case of the Labourers in Husbandry.*[2] In 1787 Davies had investigated six typical laboring families, making statistics on their incomes and expenses. These tables showed that families living on the strictest economy were inevitably running behind a little each week. Indifferently fed, badly clothed, their children without shoes and stockings and very few put to schools, most families in debt to little shopkeepers—these were the conditions Davies observed among the laborers, even though the men were working continually and the women were always busy baking, mending, and caring for children. Thelwall reminds the reader that "Citizen" Davies was not a dangerous Jacobin but a minister of religion, the rector of Barkham in Berkshire. "In visiting the labouring families of my parish, as my duty led me," Davies had written, "I could not but observe with concern their mean and distressed condition."[3]

One particular observation of Thelwall's on the agricultural revolution should be noted. Good roads and canals accompanied the expansion in agriculture. Canals in particular seem to have been as much a feature

9. *Tribune,* II, 16–17.
1. *Idem,* Vol. II, No. 25, pp. 232–3.
2. Vol. II, No. 30, pp. 321–42. Davies' work is made use of by another liberal poet, George Dyer, in his book, *The Complaints of the Poor People of England* (1793). Incidentally, Dyer (p. 73) quotes from the *Deserted Village,* as Thelwall repeatedly does.
3. *Tribune,* Vol. II, No. 30, p. 330.

of the agricultural expansion of the eighteenth century as railroads were of the manufacturing developments in the nineteenth century. Mantoux says England had not a single canal before 1759.[4] In the next thirty years the countryside was to be covered with them. Lecky, in describing this significant development, refers to Miss Aikin's *Poems* of 1773.

Miss Aiken described in graceful verse the new charm which was added to the English landscape by the silver line of placid water which relieved and brightened the barren and gloomy moor, while white sails might be seen gleaming through the dusky trees, or moving like swans in their flight, far above the traveller's head.[5]

Thelwall, the radical, sees the canal in a different way. He speaks of one newly built, which he came across in the course of an excursion in Wales.

All the fruit are conveyed to London to be consumed by the luxury of the rich, without a compensating rise of wages for agricultural labourers. . . . Twenty-one workmen were killed in digging the tunnel, and nearly 100 persons at different times drowned in the canal since cut. . . . All sorts of wickedness—thefts, licentiousness—are practised in the tunnel.[6]

After an active career as radical, Thelwall retired in 1797 to a little farm "in the obscure and romantic village of *Llys-Wen,* in Brecknockshire" on the Wye.[7] During this pastoral interlude he was rather closely associated with Coleridge and also Wordsworth, whose "Tintern Abbey" was occasioned by a visit made to Thelwall's farm. Thelwall was now devoting himself to farming and to poetry, composing his *Poems Chiefly Written in Retirement* which were published in 1801. In these verses we have the familiar themes of Wordsworth's nature poetry, such as disappointment in the world of men, nature, imagination, memory, joy. Not only are the themes here but also that faint Miltonic blank verse which Wordsworth used to give dignity and religious overtone to the subject of nature. The question of priority is fascinating, but it is not very likely that Thelwall, who had so much eighteenth-century powder in his earlier poetry, initiated such themes and such a manner. But that he gave Wordsworth economic and social knowledge can hardly be doubted.

An understanding of the agricultural revolution comparable to that of Bewick and Thelwall is revealed in the work of the poet John Clare, who was born in 1793 at Helpstone, a "gloomy village in Northamptonshire, on the brink of the Lincolnshire fens."[8] Here Clare was to live

4. Mantoux, p. 124.   5. Lecky, VI, 214.
6. Quoted from MS, in Charles Cestre, *John Thelwall* (London, Swan Sonnenschein, 1906), p. 62.
7. See *idem,* pp. 140 ff.; also see John Thelwall, *Poems Chiefly Written in Retirement* (Hereford, 1801), Prefatory Memoir, pp. xxxv ff.
8. *Sketches in the Life of John Clare,* Edmund Blunden, ed. (London, Cobden-Sanderson, 1931), p. 45.

as laborer, gardener, and cottager until fame took him momentarily into the London world of Lamb and his circle. But literature would not provide him a living, and farming remained his occupation until the breakdown which eventually confined him to the Northampton Asylum. As a boy, Clare had been given the simple and familiar literary diet for rustics. His father read the Bible but also shared his mother's enthusiasm for "the superstitious tales that are hawked about a street for a penny, such as old Nixon's Prophesies, Mother Bunches Fairy Tales, and Mother Shipton's Legacy . . ."⁹ His father was likewise fond of ballads, and Clare writes, "I have heard him make a boast of it over his horn of ale, with his merry companions, that he coud [sic] sing or recite above a hundred . . ."¹ Clare tells us that at the age of thirteen he himself had read nothing but sixpenny romances, like "Cinderella," "Little Red Ridinghood," "Jack and the Beanstalk," "Zig Zag," and "Prince Cherry."² And then, almost by accident, he discovered English poetry.

This summer I met with a fragment of Thomson's Seasons, a young man, by trade a weaver, much older than myself, then in the village, show'd it me. I knew nothing of blank verse, nor rhyme either, otherwise than by the trash of Ballad Singers, but I still remember my sensations in reading the opening of Spring. I can't say the reason, but the following lines made my heart twitter with joy:

> Come gentle Spring, ethereal mildness come
> And from the bosom of yon dropping cloud,
> While music wakes around, veil'd in a shower
> Of shadowing roses on our plains descend.³

Then follows the account of his buying and reading his copy of Thomson. The price of a copy, he understood from the weaver, who incidentally was a Methodist and preferred Wesley's hymns to Thomson, was 1s. 6d. On Sunday (and Sundays were used by Clare already for reading in secret nooks in the woods and meadows) he walked to Stamford to purchase his Thomson, but a young man in the street, who had a copy of Collins' Odes and Poems in his hand, told him the booksellers would not open their stores on Sunday for him. So on his first free weekday he returned and bought the Thomson, 6d. cheaper than he had expected. Starting for home, he couldn't wait to read his book, but he was ashamed of being seen, since a liking for books was in his village considered a form of laziness. So "I clumb [sic] over the wall into Burghley Park, and nestled in a lawn at the wall side."⁴ Thomson made Clare a poet. Immediately, in the summer of 1806, he began writing verse descriptive of the English countryside.

And a major theme of his poetry is a lament for the enclosure of the

9. *Idem,* p. 46.   1. *Ibid.*   2. *Idem,* pp. 51-2,
3. *Idem,* p. 57.   4. *Idem,* p. 59.

commons. This is the subject of such poems as "Helpstone," "Help-stone Green," "Cowper Green," "Lament of Swordy Well," the Fairy-ring sonnets, "The Fens," "Remembrances," and "The Flitting."[5] But Clare occupies an almost unique place among the poets of the village by reason of his unconcern for the peasant, for whom he had few romantic feelings. In "The Village Minstrel," a long poem describing the growth of his poetic soul, Clare, in the character of Lubin, pictures himself as a star that dwells apart. While the villagers regard Lubin as crazy, he is living largely to himself, finding enough in the village, aside from the people, to interest him in his solitary walks, his searchings for butter-flies, insects, and wild flowers. By village firesides he hears from old wives of Jack the Giant Killer, Cinderella, Tom Thumb,[6] and he listens with pleasure to the ballads sung by the homeward-wending rustics— "Peggy Band" and "Sweet Month of May."[7] The harvest home, when the last wagon comes in decorated with boughs, is a feast so attractive that Lubin joins with the "low vulgar crew" in their mirth.[8] But to Lubin the general vulgarity of the hinds, clowns, and louts of the village is apparent enough. Dick takes Dolly to a rout, buys her some ribbons, and on the way home at night expects to be paid for the entertainment.[9] Dolly murmurs something about the dew's spoiling her Sunday gown, but there her resistance ends. Clare poses as a superior soul, if in real life his conduct was not so unlike that of Dick or Hodge.

It is appropriate that Thomson should have been the poetic begetter of Clare, for Clare is a nature poet, more attracted to the fields and their flowers than to the life of man. Clare mourns the commons, not because they had been the home of an ideal race of men, but because they represented to him Nature—nature in her "wildness and variety." Natural beauty disappeared when enclosure leveled the fields, straight-ened the streams or shut them off, cleared the thin-scattered bushes, hanged the much-loved mole, cut down the trees, and generally civilized and utilized this wild old neglected common, moor, heath. Eye and ear have been great losers by enclosure. Primrose, violet, anemone.

> Like mighty giants of their limbs bereft,
> The skybound wastes in mangled garbs are left,
> Fence meeting fence in owner's little bounds
> Of field and meadow, large as garden-grounds,
> In little parcels little minds to please . . .[1]

Skylark, blackcap, moor hen, willow biter.

> Enclosure like a Buonaparte let not a thing remain,
> It levelled every bush and tree and levelled every hill

5. *The Poems of John Clare,* J. W. Tibble, ed. (London, J. M. Dent & Sons, 1935. 2 vols.), I, 3, 35, 174, 420; II, 138 ff., 278, 257, 251.
6. *Idem,* I, 144.   7. *Idem,* I, 145.
8. *Idem,* I, 145–6.   9. *Idem,* I, 150.
1. "Enclosure," *idem,* I, 420.

And hung the moles for traitors—though the brook is running still
It runs a naked stream, cold and chill.[2]

Obviously, Clare has chosen to mourn the plumage and forget the dying bird. His attitude toward the agricultural revolution may be likened to that of William Hutchinson, author of the well-known *Excursion to the Lakes,* who was disturbed because improvement was destroying the ancient monuments and ruins to which he as a lover of the picturesque was devoted![3]

6. *"A Bold Peasantry"*

Direct opposition to the agricultural revolution is less pronounced in creative work devoted to the peasant than one might perhaps expect or wish. But we may say nonetheless that, wherever the peasant was idealized, there the artistic movement set itself against the agricultural revolution, and this may occur in work which ignored social decay or misrepresented its causes as well as in work which seemed to be set justly in the social scene. This was the real contribution of the imagination to a good cause. We may turn, then, for a moment to consider this image of the peasant which emerged in the literature and art of these years. Writers like Cowper and Crabbe, who did not share the romantic feelings of their day for the peasant, will drop out of our discussion, while at the same time we may speak of other work which did not seem to call for any particular economic comment.

It is, I think, significant that in so many handlings of the peasant there is little if any repetition of the sentiments which Gray had expressed in his otherwise prophetic *Elegy Written in a Country Churchyard* of 1751.[4] Gray interpreted the peasant in terms of the classic ideal. Far

2. "Remembrances," *idem,* II, 259.
3. William Hutchinson, *Excursion to the Lakes in Westmoreland and Cumberland, with a Tour through Part of the Northern Counties, in the Years 1773 and 1774* (London, 1776), p. 2.
4. Thomas Day's *Sanford and Merton* may be an exception. The Reverend Mr. Barlow, who helps in the reformation of young Merton, holds the Roman example before the

from the ignoble strife of the madding crowd, these rude sons of toil
realized in their lives a golden mean, keeping an even, undisturbed
tenor in their being. In one way they are contrasted with the great, who
are disturbed by ambition, and in another way with the distressed poet
himself, whom melancholy has marked for its own. It is, I think, a fair
supposition that the rural ideal, classically conceived, had been so
definitely identified by the end of the century with the activities of the
gentleman farmer that it could not be, and would not be, used in the
depiction of the peasant.[5]

In the art and literature of this period we may detect several conventional approaches to the peasant character, and one of these interpreta-
tions is set directly against the view of the peasant presented by Gray.
Both Burns and Wordsworth give us a peasant who, far from possessing
composure, exhibits the passions in their fullest and most elementary
form. What Burns's lyrics told his age was that romantic love in its
full glory belonged to the peasant world. This, to be sure, is an old
pastoral idea, but it comes with a new force and vividness in the Burns
song.

> It was upon a Lammas night,
> When corn rigs are bonie,
> Beneath the moon's unclouded light,
> I held awa to Annie;

---

indulged young man: "When the Roman people, oppressed by their enemies, were
looking out for a leader, able to defend them and change the fortune of the war, where did
they seek for this extraordinary man? It was neither at banquets, nor in splendid palaces,
nor amid the gay, the elegant, or the dissipated; they turned their steps towards a poor
and solitary cottage, such as the meanest of your late companions would consider with
contempt; there they found Cincinnatus, whose virtues and abilities were allowed to
excel all the rest of his citizens, turning up the soil with a pair of oxen, and holding the
plough himself." Thomas Day, *History of Sanford and Merton* (London, 1783–89. 3
vols.), III, 274. But Day's ideal, influenced as it was by the educational writings of
Locke and Rousseau, was hardly the classical golden mean: it was Spartan, rather. Barlow crams young Merton with accounts of one bleak civilization after another—Spartan,
Scythian, American Indian, Scottish Highlander. These histories are supplemented
by stories of the self-help of Robinson Crusoe and of four Russian sailors stranded
upon an Arctic island.

5. Wordsworth has a poem entitled "To the Spade of a Friend (an Agriculturist)," addressed to Thomas Wilkinson and composed while the poet was helping this friend in
his pleasure ground at his farm on the banks of the Emont flowing out of Ullswater.
Wordsworth describes Wilkinson's way of living in the language of the golden mean,
saying that it combines

> . . . the best of high and low,
> The labouring many and the resting few . . .

It is the perfectly balanced life, which makes for emotional balance. Wordsworth gives a
classical reading of the rural life of the gentleman, but peasant life he interprets quite
otherwise. His practice illustrates a distinction which seems generally to have been
observed in his day. See Wordsworth, *Poetical Works*, pp. 489–90, and *Early Letters*,
p. 526.

The time flew by, wi' tentless heed;
Till, 'tween the late and early,
Wi' sma' persuasion she agreed
To see me thro' the barley.[6]

It is quite proper that Currie, Burns's biographer, should accept this romantic interpretation of the peasant character in his essay on the Scottish peasantry which introduces his study of the poet published in 1800. To Currie the great sanctuaries of romantic love were the pastoral lands of Scotland, Cumberland, Switzerland, and (what is most surprising) New England! He quotes the following remark of Burns on the loves of the peasant: "To the sons and daughters of labour and poverty they are matters of the most serious nature; to them the ardent hope, the stolen interview, the tender farewell, are the greatest and most delicious parts of their enjoyments."[7]

The ardent love life of Cumberland, one of Currie's sanctuaries, was shortly to be reported by Thomas Sanderson in notes he contributed to Robert Anderson's *Ballads in the Cumberland Dialect* (Carlisle, 1805). To keep a nocturnal engagement, a Cumbrian peasant, Sanderson reports, may walk in the dark ten or twelve miles over the worst kind of country. When he knocks on the pane, his beloved dresses and descends, and stealthily admits him to the kitchen, where she serves her lover the almost Keatsian luxuries of the Cumbrian cottage—cream and sugared curds. The fire is then darkened, and the pair make love till

6. *The Complete Poetical Works of Robert Burns*, W. E. Henley, ed. (Cambridge ed. Boston, Houghton Mifflin, 1897), p. 51.

7. *The Works of Robert Burns*, I, 46. Currie seems to have accepted completely and entirely the rural convention of his time. In his biography of Burns (1800) (the second edition of which had a frontispiece portrait of Burns flanked by bagpipes, rake, and sickle) one is tempted to see a document in late eighteenth-century rusticity. Currie tells really the story of a peasant of the soil who was strong and virtuous until his middle twenties, when he went to Edinburgh and, like Michael's son, went to pieces. Burns left for Edinburgh in November, 1786, and then, in the words of Currie, the "melancholy record" follows. *Idem*, I, 130. Dugald Stewart, who, meeting Burns in the country, saw in him a wonderful native simplicity, manliness, and independence (*idem*, I, 136), said of his coming to Edinburgh, ". . . I dreaded the consequences . . ." *Idem*, I, 137. Few peasants could have given more satisfactory and immediate evidence of the ill effect of a "sedentary and luxurious life" than Burns. After a winter in Edinburgh Burns announced to the horrified Dugald Stewart that he had developed a palpitation of the heart! *Idem*, I, 141.

But Burns did not lose in the city all memory of former innocence! In Edinburgh he saw Dugald Stewart occasionally, but not so often as the philosopher would perhaps have wished. His time was spent much in the company of the unphilosophical. But once or twice he walked with Stewart early in the morning in the direction of Braid-Hills, the scenery of which had inspired Fergusson's poem, "Written at the Hermitage of Braid." On these walks, Stewart was more than ever charmed by the conversation of the poet. Stewart writes: "He was passionately fond of the beauties of nature; and I recollect once he told me, when I was admiring a distant prospect in one of our morning walks, that the sight of so many smoking cottages gave a pleasure to his mind, which none could understand who had not witnessed, like himself, the happiness and the worth which they contained." *Idem*, I, 138–9. Wordsworth knew this story. See *Prose Works*, I, 355–6.

dawn. These meetings at night, we are told, were generally restricted
to the week end. While Sanderson is quick to point out the grave dangers
to morality of this ancient custom, still he cannot but praise the love
of these Cumberland peasants, whose strong passions were their pre-
rogative and their excuse. "The passion of love," he writes elsewhere,
"restrained by forms and ceremonies in the higher classes of society,
breaks out in all its vehemence in the breast of a simple, uneducated
Cumbrian peasant."[8]

The concept of the romantic peasant was widely diffused in this period,
and I think we must suppose that it was particularly the lyrics of Burns
which established this view of things.

Wordsworth's peasant world was likewise one of passion. In the
Preface of 1800 Wordsworth has said that the affections, which in
sophisticated urban society are continually suppressed and hidden,
develop freely and fully among peoples living simple and rather solitary
lives on the land. But Wordsworth is thinking not particularly of love
but of all the affections. To all of them belongs that intensity which
Burns gives principally to romantic passion. With all the affections so
tuned, Wordsworth's peasant world becomes the scene of tragic experience, for here there is the continual possibility that one strong affection will come into conflict with another. The tragic character of peasant
life Wordsworth has best recreated in "Michael," where we see a struggle
between a man's love of his son and his love of inherited property, with
the less worthy feeling controlling finally his actions.

Passion was but one of the rich possessions of the peasant world as
it was interpreted in this period. That the peasant was also creative in
the ways of lovely poetry and myth is an impression which could not
be held back when the country ballad came to receive such attention as
it did in the last years of the eighteenth century. The enthusiasm of
the scholars and poets for popular rural poetry, just at the time when
the rural world was experiencing social stress, did not surely derive
from this economic circumstance, though devotees of the ballad must
frequently have recognized the elegiac character of their taste. But, with
or without an economic awareness on the part of its preservers, the
ballad had great social meaning in a time when the cottage was disappearing. It was sign and seal of the aesthetic character of the inhabitants of these vanishing cottages.

To the romantics the ballad represented pure poetry,[9] and this pure
poetry, when all others were unfaithful, had been preserved by the simple
people of England's farm world. Loved by lord and man alike in the

8. Sanderson's note, No. 12.
9. "Since the coming of Romanticism the debt of literature to the ballad has been
comparable to that of the Renaissance to the Greek and Latin classics . . ." W. J. Entwistle, *European Balladry* (Oxford, Clarendon Press, 1939), p. 119.

hearty days of the sixteenth century, the ballad lost its social place with the rise of English Renaissance literature and the great drama of the Elizabethans. Shakespeare made a little use of it in his plays, but significantly in scenes of pathos such as before Desdemona's death and after Ophelia's madness—tender scenes which somehow express as much the plight of the poor ballad as of the sad ladies themselves. The neoclassical period produced a literature still more refined than the Elizabethan, with no room at all for country song. In this night of sophistication the ballad retired to "the fastnesses of hearth and barn" and there, like a king in disguise, lived on until it was called forth to provide something more simple, sensuous, and passionate than the standards of neoclassicism had allowed.[1] By love and memory, the ballad was preserved during the dark age by the simple folk of English hearth and ingle, whose sure natural senses understood "true poetry"! Indeed, the activities of Burns and Scott and others in going directly to the peasantry to get this poetry, pointed out who were the real men of taste.[2]

1. The change of taste in favor of the ballad is nicely dramatized in Day's *History of Sanford and Merton*. In this story of the reformation of Playboy Tommy Merton through the influence of Plowboy Harry Sanford, the boys return on one occasion to the Merton home for a house party with other young people. Plowboy Harry finds himself completely miserable among these snobbish friends of Tommy who are as soft and foppish as Tommy once had been. Their dinner parties, balls, cards, and polite conversation about actresses bore the virtuous Plowboy to extinction. He is as uncomfortable as Huck Finn in the pious parlor of the Widow Douglas. Only one girl at the party pays attention to the Plowboy, and that is Sukey Simmons, a well-born little lady like the rest, who however had been brought up *à-la-Rousseau*. She "was accustomed from her earliest years to plunge into the cold bath at every season of the year, to rise by candle-light in winter, to ride a dozen miles upon a trotting horse, or to walk as many even with the hazard of being splashed or soiling her clothes." II, 226. On one occasion at the house party Sukey sings for the crowd "a little Scotch song, called Lochaber" (II, 238), which moves Harry indeed but leaves the little snobs completely cold, who prefer Italian music, and singing of the *virtuoso* variety.

2. It was part of Wordsworth's credo that "simple and unadulterated minds" had "a sense of the beautiful and sublime in art." *Letters . . . Middle Years*, I, 371. Accordingly he read "Resolution and Independence" to his barber to get his opinion! *Early Letters*, pp. 303–4. The natural good taste of the cottager is the theme of this little poem, written in 1803.

> Who fancied what a pretty sight
> This Rock would be if edged around
> With living snow-drops? circlet bright!
> How glorious to this orchard-ground!
> Who loved the little Rock, and set
> Upon its head this coronet?
>
> Was it the humour of a child?
> Or rather of some gentle maid,
> Whose brows, the day that she was styled
> The shepherd-queen, were thus arrayed?
> Of man mature, or matron sage?
> Or old man toying with his age?
>
> I asked—'twas whispered; The device
> To each and all might well belong:

The rural world was not only to be credited with the preservation of the ballads but also, more important, with their composition. It was a joy past belief to think that not only had these romantic peasants preserved this pure poetry, but that in some mystical medieval way the heart and mind of the peasantry, the people, had united in the composition of these ballads. Percy, publishing in 1765, did not accept this bewildering theory; nor is it entertained by modern students of the ballad.[3] In the first critical essay in the *Reliques,* entitled "Essay on the Ancient Minstrels in England," Percy presents historically the career of the minstrel class who were, he supposes, generally the composers and singers of the ballad. But not long after Percy, opinion began to favor the notion that the ballads were a creation of the folk mind.[4] The romantic Andrew Lang, writing as late as 1910 for the eleventh edition of the *Encyclopaedia Britannica,* still sought to prove that, like the fairy tales of Cinderella and the Sleeping Beauty, the ballads were born "from the lips and heart of the people."[5] But Lang himself admitted that it was a much exaggerated opinion that a whole people composed its own ballads. The theory, he allowed, could be accepted only imaginatively, not literally.

The ballads were suggestive of another creative power of the country mind, by reason of the folklore and popular mythology present in so many of them. The rural mind had created Robin Goodfellow, the merry prankster who is always pinching lazy maids in bed, misleading night wanderers with his call, or misbehaving vulgarly at parties. And out of rural fancy had come the fairy queen who dances with her train upon the green and dines with them by moonlight upon a mushroom's head, on brains of nightingales, tails of worms, marrow of mice, while grasshopper, gnat, and fly make dinner music. The suggestions the ballad offers about this imaginative aspect of the country mind were not taken up in English literature quite to the extent they might have been. Only once, in his "Idiot Boy," did Wordsworth deal more than casually with rural folklore, and his dealing was such as to suggest that the poet himself had perhaps been tricked by Robin Goodfellow.[6] Scott was en-

---

It is the Spirit of Paradise
That prompts such work, a Spirit strong,
That gives to all the self-same bent
Where life is wise and innocent.

3. Entwistle says that the ballads were the work of "professionals," that there is no basis for "the mystical doctrine of people's authorship." For his rejection of the romantic theory, see *European Balladry,* pp. 10 ff., 28 ff.
4. See Francis B. Gummere, *Beginnings of Poetry* (New York, Macmillan, 1901), pp. 128 ff.   5. Article on "Ballads."
6. There are, of course, in Wordsworth many incidental uses of such folklore, especially in the group, "Poems of the Fancy." See Wordsworth, *Poetical Works,* pp. 159, 160, 162, 163, 164. See too the beginning of Canto Fourth of *The Waggoner* and the poem "A Whirlblast from behind the Hill" (1798).

thusiastic about country myth and wrote the excellent essay "On the Fairies of Popular Superstition."[7] But these treasures of the rural world it was left very much to the Continent to develop.

Irving contributed rather uniquely to the concept of the aesthetic peasant. In his *Sketch Book* he has given us a peasantry whose life is rich with the beauty of rural ceremony—its Christmas observances, its lovely services for marriage and burial. In his pages we see a rural world of ritual and custom as pretty and as varied as an old-fashioned nosegay. To sense the beauty of Irving's village of Maypoles and flower-burials, we need only contrast Miss Mitford's cheery little middle-class village, addicted to sewing, morning calling, and jams and jellies. I think it is remarkable that Irving, writing at the end of a tradition when nearly fifty years had been devoted to the interpretation of the peasant, should have found such fresh material. His fortune depended partly, it would seem, upon his having ignored altogether the contemporary facts of his rural world, to go back to the village of Herrick and Shakespeare. Few if any of these customs survived in his time.

> This, alas!
> Was but a dream; the times had scatter'd all
> These lighter graces, and the rural custom
> And manners which it was my chance to see
> In childhood were severe and unadorn'd,
> The unluxuriant produce of a life
> Intent on little but substantial needs,
> Yet beautiful, and beauty that was felt.[8]

Thus Wordsworth wrote in the *Prelude* as he reflected upon the old rural world of interesting manners and customs—the songs, the Maying, the decorated churches. Perhaps Irving makes silent confession of this truth in the particular attention he gives to the flower ceremonies for the burial of the maiden.

In the composite portrait of the peasant which emerges in the literature and art of the period, there are contradictions, and these exist often within the work of the single person. While Burns in his lyrics has given us the image of a peasant most capable of romantic love, elsewhere and more often he has shown rustic energy moving into coarser channels, dissipating itself in hard drinking, rowdyism, lewdness. Henley saw principally these qualities in Burns's peasantry, whom he describes as "poor-living, lewd, grimy, free-spoken, ribald."[9] Such a peasantry we see in "Holy Fair"; they go to the church fair for the

7. "Introduction to the Tale of Tamlane," *Minstrelsy of the Scottish Border,* T. Henderson, ed. (New York, Thomas Y. Crowell, 1931), pp. 288–327.

8. *Prelude* (1805–6), Ernest de Selincourt, ed. (Oxford, Clarendon Press, 1926), Bk. VIII, ll. 203 ff.

9. *The Complete Poetical Works of Robert Burns,* p. xxii.

preaching, but also for a day of drinking and, after dark, "hough-magandie." "Halloween," prefaced with lines from the *Deserted Village,* is only a slightly more innocent picture of the peasant, whose super-stitions Burns is here exploring, with footnotes. On such a night the pulling of a cabbage root may tell what one's husband and offspring will be like. But these charms seem a little *post facto* for young people who retire intermittently to the cornstalks, or fause-house, for their love-making. These are Breughel's muscular, thick-legged, thick-headed peasants—always fascinating to any unenergetic society. It was Burns especially who created for his time the image of a rough, animalistic peasantry, wonderful for its lustiness and energy.

Wordsworth was, to be sure, unwilling to see his northern peasantry in this light, save perhaps in one instance, when he is describing the merry-night in his *Waggoner.*[1] Here he pictures the rude vigor of a midnight country dance at the Cherry Tree Inn, where Ben and the sailor stop with the wain for a drink and a dance—where the sailor produces his large model of the Flagship of the Nile before the wondering eyes of the rustics. This was quite a night for Ben, and also for Words-worth! It didn't happen again. But there was another lesser known poet of the Lake District who made himself a disciple of the realistic Burns. This was Robert Anderson (1770–1833), who in 1805 pub-lished his *Ballads in the Cumberland Dialect.* A second edition in 1815 carried an appropriate frontispiece showing a country fellow about to be led inside by an urban courtesan. Lines printed beneath read:

> A wheyte-feac'd young Lass, aw dess'd out leyke a Leady
> Cried "pray Sir step in!" but I wish I'd kept out!

Anderson's Cumberland peasants are rough and vulgar, always capable of drunkenness, immorality, brawling. Whatever Anderson touches turns to a fight. Be it a wedding ("The Worton Weddin"), or the races ("Burgh Races"), or a house-raising ("The Clay Daubin"), the rustic affair ends in a free-for-all of the local yokels, with sweethearts some-times taking a hand. There are, it is true, tales of true love in these ballads, but somehow one is more impressed with the numerous stories of daring infidelity. The swain in love with Barbary Bell steals to her cottage window at night and there espies his beloved engaged with Watty, a local laird.

> That varra seame neet, up to Barbary's house,
>   When aw t' auld swok were liggin asleep,
> I off wi' my clogs, and as whisht as a mouse,
>   Claver'd up to the window, and tuik a peep;
> There whee sud I see, but Watty the laird—

---

1. Canto Second, ll. 30 ff., in Wordsworth, *Poetical Works,* pp. 177–8.

The dialect Anderson has preserved in the Cumberland ballads only accentuates the coarseness and hardness of his country clowns, whose blows and kisses crack like waggoners' whips. It is interesting to think that at the very time when Wordsworth was formulating his nice theories about the Lake country peasantry, another poet, just over the hills in another valley, was working in such a different spirit.[2]

In his volumes on quadrupeds, birds, etc., Thomas Bewick used as end pieces hundreds of engravings of scenes from simple rural life, the life of small farmers and cottagers. Today these end pieces are surely regarded as the most interesting part of his work as an artist. Bewick again pictures a peasantry that is rough and rude, but with a difference. His country world is not, like Anderson's, simply drunken and brawling. It is rough rather in the ways of slapstick comedy, and those who know country life may feel that Bewick has struck upon great truth. A few of these end pieces might be quickly mentioned. In the volume of *Land Birds* are pictures of a runaway horse with cart full of frightened children; a country fellow riding a pig barefoot and bareback, having a wonderful time; another asleep under a bush on "4 June 1795"; an old shaggy, large-jawed, toothless fisherman whose dog mo-

2. Strangely enough, Anderson's first poetical work, "Lucy Gray," is thought to have been the inspiration of Wordsworth's ballad sequence. The story of Lucy (a village beauty who died in her seventeenth year) Anderson is supposed to have heard from a Northumberland rustic. See *DNB*, under Anderson.

Anderson apparently collected manuscript poems of a fellow poet of Cumberland, Susanna Blamire (1747–94), whose work was largely unpublished until 1842. *The Poetical Works of Miss Susanna Blamire*, Henry Lonsdale, ed., with Preface, Memoir, and Notes by Patrick Maxwell (Edinburgh, 1842). Miss Blamire was very much of a lady, with fine country connections, but she had a side to her nature which led her to go to "merry neets" where she danced with the bashful villagers, who thought her "a bonny and varra lish young lass." *Idem*, p. xxiii. Such experience gave her an insight into the real lives of Cumberland peasants. She draws lively pictures of their country fairs and dances. In "The Cumberland Scold" and "Barley Broth" we have especially fine, realistic scenes from domestic life. One sees in her "Songs in the Cumberland Dialect" a peasantry akin to that of the harder Burns.

lests a bull from a plank across the narrow stream. This is Bewick's bull with the wise eyes, who appears in other plates. To see him once is always to remember him. Other plates in *Land Birds* show pictures of an old loafer fishing from his horse amid stream; a big-jawed rustic carrying his like across a bog; a country fellow sitting in a wheelbarrow smoking his pipe; a cottage wife spreading clothes to dry, not seeing the pigs and chickens entering the gate just left open by departing visitors; workers watching a dog with a tin can on his tail; a horse grazing with a basket tied to his buttocks to catch manure; a traveler on a horse beset by bees; "stupid" carrying a bird cage in the snow; some thirty country fellows standing at the end of a rainbow![3] In the end pieces of *Water Birds,* to mention but a few, we see the bull attacking a fisherman cornered by the stream; children riding tombstones like hobbyhorses in a country graveyard; a rude fellow urinating by a wall.[4] *Quadrupeds* has such pictures as that of a child pulling a stallion's tail with mother rushing, nearly mad, from a ladder near by; a sow being driven along with string tied to a back leg.[5] In *Aesop* there are pictures of a country fellow trying to catch a nag in the meadow with his cap; of the great bull driving a boy up a tree; of a drunkard on his way home seeing two moons![6] The social interest of some of the plates which show interiors and exteriors of cottages and farmhouses cannot be overstated.

One should say, in conclusion, that there is more than just humor in Bewick's peasant world, for into his rough-and-ready country occasionally peep terror and catastrophe. Sometimes we see mad fellows being driven by devils to hang themselves. And there are corpses hanging, Housman-like, on gallows. Here is slapstick of quite a different kind.

The artist George Morland, whose short life ended in 1804, did thousands of paintings of subjects generally rural and generally humble, if not low.[7] What one notices particularly in these pictures is the animals. We are told that in his prosperous days Morland was always bringing home pigs, fowl, and rabbits. He liked dogs and horses, but pigs were rather his speciality.[8] Animal existence becomes the subplot of his painting, paralleling the story of man. The dog watches and smells the cooking on the grate. Pigs begin to stir in their straw and look for food as the village higglers get up from their straw and drink before going to market. The gipsy-father sleeps in the woods with his family, and the dog sleeps beside him. The donkey and the fisherman each carries his burden. Carriers sleep in the stable beside their horses. This dungy earth feeds man and beast alike. More clearly than Burns or Bewick,

3. *Memorial Edition of Thomas Bewick's Works* (Newcastle-upon-Tyne, 1885–87. 5 vols.), I, 35, 47, 82, 149, 256, 176, 203, 237, 275, 298, 310, 362, 332.
    4. *Idem,* II, 20, 244, 105.   5. *Idem,* III, 15, 165.   6. *Idem,* IV, 56, 312, 242.
    7. George Dawe, *Life of George Morland.* Illustrated. With Introduction and Notes by J. J. Foster (London, Dickinsons, 1904), p. 97.
    8. *Idem,* pp. 44, 105.

Morland sees the affinity of humble country life to animal life, and the association is a sad one. Rustic life, indeed, would seem to fulfill the worst part of human sadness, and this his well-shadowed canvases tell us.

Another interpretation of the character of the peasant we have waited to the last to mention, for it is this reading of the peasant which probably comes so often to mind as to make one forget all other readings. This is the view that the peasant possesses superior virtue, that he is in fact an innocent. If this sentimental peasant is unpalatable wherever he appears, he is less offending in some instances than in others. In the case of the *Deserted Village,* which did much to start this theme, the innocence of Goldsmith's beautiful people seems to imply a kind of helplessness. His memorable phrase, "a bold peasantry," unfortunately does not apply to his own villagers of Auburn, who impress us as being a simple, "vacant" people, who would be rather put to it without their spiritual and intellectual mentors, their priests and schoolmasters. They lack boldness, and Goldsmith makes them appear incapable of dealing with anything so harsh as the wild landscape of blazing suns and rank vegetation to which they are to be exposed when they leave the kind fields of England. Thomas Day has given us quite a different picture of rustic virtue in his boys' serial, *Sanford and Merton* (1783–89). Day was a disciple of Rousseau, and Rousseau was, we must remember, the real founder of the Boy Scouts. In the person of Harry Sanford, who redeems Tommy Merton from society and softness, Day has pictured rustic virtue in combination with preparedness and priggishness, thus quite reversing Goldsmith. Much more successful presentation of rural innocence we find in the work of Gainsborough[9] and Blake, who in developing this theme wisely chose in the cottage world to concentrate upon the image of the child. In so doing they found the perfect symbol of their idea, and at the same time they avoided the problem of social capacity. But both Gainsborough and Blake had something more to offer than a good image of innocence. Gainsborough's pictures of the cottage child, such as that of little Jack Hill warming his hands before the fire, revealed an almost Franciscan sense of the beauty of the poverty upon which rustic innocence depends. And Blake, describing

9. Of Gainsborough, Uvedale Price wrote: "Though of a lively and playful imagination, yet was he at times severe and sarcastic, but when we have come near to cottages and village scenes with groups of children, and objects of rural life that struck his fancy, I have observed his countenance to take an expression of gentleness and complacency." Quoted in C. B. Tinker, *Painter and Poet* (Cambridge, Mass., Harvard University Press, 1938), p. 88, from W. T. Whitley, *Thomas Gainsborough* (1915), p. 41. "If I can pick pockets in the portrait way two or three years longer," Gainsborough once wrote, "I intend to sneak into a cot, and turn a serious fellow." Quoted in *idem,* p. 88, from Whitley, p. 204. Gainsborough never sneaked into a cot, but he had the pleasure of painting many cottage pictures. As early as the seventies he was doing such studies. The date of the "Cottage-Door" is 1778. The next decade saw "The Shepherd-Boy in a Storm," "Girl and Pigs," "Peasants at a Grave," and other rural paintings.

rural innocence, showed a profound understanding of the character of innocence. His innocence is benevolence, pity, sympathy.

> Can I see another's woe,
> And not be in sorrow too?
> Can I see another's grief,
> And not seek for kind relief?

Evil, or experience, he interprets as self-interest.

> Nought loves another as itself . . .

The *Songs of Innocence and Experience* would seem to have been deeply set in the ethics of the eighteenth-century moralists who propounded these two contrasting ethical theories.

These then, to conclude, are some of the features we find in that composite portrait of the peasant which was created by literature and painting during the period which saw the destruction of peasant life. This combined image of the peasant, exhibiting, indeed, so many valuable characteristics of mind and heart, constituted, one must feel, a proper challenge and rebuttal to the agricultural revolution and its indifference, its hostility to peasant life. The poets and artists found their mark, even though many of them seem to have been firing very much in the dark.

7. Epilogue

The great landholders were not suffering in the years that were hard on peasant and laborer. The era of the Napoleonic wars saw for them the culmination of a period of prosperity which began about 1785. The Hammonds say that rents in England increased in some cases as much as fivefold between 1790 and 1812.[1] Toynbee records that a farm in Essex which rented for 10*s.* an acre before 1793, in 1812 brought 50*s.* an acre.[2] In Scotland, according to Hamilton, rents had increased 150 per cent by the end of the Napoleonic wars.[3] These high rents were paid

1. Hammond, p. 151.   2. Toynbee, p. 92.   3. Hamilton, p. 74.

by the big farmers who prospered in equal measure. In 1793 Sir John Sinclair printed the following cheery verses in the *Annals of Agriculture,* under the title "The Farmer's Creed."[4]

> Let this be held the farmer's creed.—
> For stock seek out the choicest breed,
> In peace and plenty let them feed;
> Your land sow with the best of seed,
> Let it nor dung nor dressing need,
> Inclose and drain it with all speed,
> And you will soon be rich indeed.

Four years later the excitement of this new and great agricultural wealth caused the *Annals of Agriculture* to break forth again in verse, with the poem by Abraham Wilkinson entitled "Cultivation," addressed to his fellow poet Sir John Sinclair. The theme of this poem is the prosperity English agriculture enjoys, while wars are thinning the ranks of mankind. For all this, poetic thanks to Sir John Sinclair and the other great improvers.

> Long shall Britannia hold in mem'ry dear
> The name of Bakewell, long his worth revere,
> While her rich meads, improv'd in comely form,
> The sheep, the steer, and gen'rous steed adorn.
> No mean applause industrious Young may claim,
> Who points to British youth the path of fame;
> Nor can we soon forget a Ducket's toil,
> Whose fertile genius best subdues the soil.[5]

The appearance of a new class of rich farmers was a conspicuous social phenomenon of this prosperous period. The *Annals of Agriculture* in the splendid year of 1796 defined a farmer as one who *"does not perform manual labour."*[6] This new type of farmer had nothing in common with his simple predecessor who used to sit around the oak board on terms of equality with his laborers. The loss of this intimacy between farmer and laborer is the elegiac theme of Robert Bloomfield's *The Farmer's Boy,* a poem which, with the sponsorship of Capel Lofft, was published in 1800 in a handsome edition illustrated by Bewick. The poem describes the idyllic life of the country laborer of the past, happily employed and living on familiar terms with his master. That similar happiness is not now to be found in all such units, Robert Bloomfield strongly laments.[7] Farmers are growing rich, and with their wealth they are taking on new manners and ways of life in which their servants do not share. At harvest home no longer does the farmer sit with his laborers and drink the simple home-brewed ale; instead he now has a table apart, with special wine and special guests.

4. xx (1793), 543.   5. xxix (1797), 370.   6. xxvi (1796), 523.
7. *The Farmer's Boy* (London, 1800), pp. 45 ff.

Everywhere now was there the evidence of "conspicuous waste" among rich farmers—new furniture, new plate, and elaborate harness for the carriage. Pleasure horses multiplied enormously in this period. When finally hard times came for the farmer, he was in turn told that his standard of living, like the laborer's, was too high. Why should the farmer not feel poor, for "He now assumes the manners and demands the equipage of a gentleman, keeps a table like his landlord, anticipates seasons in their productions, is as choice in his wines, his horses, and his furniture"?[8] The enriched farmer might also share the gentleman's enthusiasm for landscape gardening, even in the picturesque manner. We have noted above that the school of the picturesque took no pleasure in cultivation, since it was lacking in wildness. But agriculture might be brought into some harmony with the demands of taste. For the *Annals of Agriculture,*[9] Thomas Ruggles of Clare, Suffolk, writes a series of essays on "Picturesque Farming," proposing methods of keeping the wildness of the picturesque in an improved farm. Since the regular oblong parallelogram was the most practical field, Ruggles suggests that the grass margin be kept "irregular" to give a rough picturesque effect. He also recommends for picturesque farming a diversified planting to give a variety in summer crops, the placing of mottoes on trees, and the painting of the instruments of husbandry—a suggestion he adopts, incidentally, from Bishop Watson.[1]

Crabbe in parts of the *Parish Register*[2] and Clare throughout his *Parish*[3] satirize the babbittry of the *nouveaux riches* farmers of this boom period. In the latter poem, Young Farmer Bigg, Young Headlong Racket, Dandy Flint, Esq., Farmer Cheetum, Old Saveall typify the class made rich by enclosure and improvement. They do not, like their humble predecessors, milk their cows and sing old ballads, but, performing no manual labor whatever, they pass their time hunting and whoring and drinking, not ale but wine. Their wives are their congenial consorts. Their daughters aspire to marry gentlemen and end up by running away with serving men.

The name of "farmer" was possibly as much scorned in the years around 1800 as that of "capitalist" in some parts of our society today. Wordsworth's "Goody Blake and Harry Gill" (1798) tells of a little old woman who lives all by herself in a cottage far from the village green. Though she spins all day, and three hours a night, she doesn't make enough to live on. Her great desideratum seems to be fuel. In summer it is lovely to sit outdoors of an evening in the bright warm

8. Quoted in Curtler, p. 264, from a work entitled *Refutation of the Arguments Used on the Subject of the Agricultural Petition* (1819).
9. *Annals,* VI (1786), 175–84; VII (1786), 20–8; VIII (1787), 89–97; IX (1788), 1–10
1. *Idem,* IX, 10.
2. *The Poetical Works of George Crabbe,* p. 56.
3. "The Parish: a Satire," *The Poems of John Clare,* I, 542 ff.

sun. But in winter she has to go to bed for the cold, and in bed she shivers. She is grateful for a winter storm that shakes down some firewood. And much does she love a hedge, like Harry Gill's where she goes to steal sticks. Unfortunately, she is caught by the owner, whom she curses. But the moral law is on her side, and prosperous Harry Gill, in spite of his abundant clothing, is never warm again. Though Gill himself is a drover, it should be noted that the last lines of this poem are a warning to farmers.

> Now think, ye farmers all, I pray,
> Of Goody Blake and Harry Gill!

The moral of the poem is shot at members of a class who at that time were in the heyday of prosperity while the poorer members of rural society were experiencing their greatest hardship.

In view of the comfort of the larger land interests during this golden age it is not pleasant to consider the decision handed down in 1788 by the Court of Common Pleas against gleaning.[4] In the year of this decision a controversy develops in the pages of the *Annals of Agriculture* between "picturesque" Ruggles and Capel Lofft. The latter, taking the side of the gleaners, appeals to the law in the Bible, the writings of Hale, Gilbert, and Blackstone,[5] and he sends us also to the *Correspondence of Henry and Frances,* Volume IV, for a picture of the virtuous gleaner.[6] "Here, if I divide against Mr. Ruggles, our common friends the *poets* and the *philosophical moralists,* at least some of the most eminent of these, and whom he esteems in proportion to their desert, will for once quit his side, and will join with the *gleaners.*"[7]

A little later an effort was made to remove the burden of the beggar from the land. Wordsworth was accordingly prompted in 1797 to write the "Old Cumberland Beggar."[8] Thinking as always in terms of association and memory, Wordsworth saw the regular appearances of the beggar on his rounds as a reminder of acts of kindness, of all kinds, not just of those to the beggar himself. His round thus served to keep all the human sympathies alive. The beggar indeed performed somewhat the same associative function as nature, being, however, just reminder and not, as nature, symbol and reminder both.

> While from door to door
> This old Man creeps, the villagers in him
> Behold a record which together binds

4. See Hammond, p. 85.   5. See *idem,* p. 84.
6. *Annals,* x (1788), 221 n.   7. *Idem,* IX (1788), 165.
8. The physiocrats in France had crusaded against the beggar. Since Wordsworth passed some time in Orléans, we are interested to read this statement in Weulersse's history of physiocracy: "La nécessité d'exterminer des campagnes les vagabonds voleurs et pilleurs est un point sur lequel le Physiocrate d'Orléans se prononça toujours avec beaucoup de force." Weulersse, I, 422–3.

Past deeds and offices of charity,
Else unremembered, and so keeps alive
The kindly mood in hearts which lapse of years,
And that half-wisdom half-experience gives,
Make slow to feel, and by sure steps resign
To selfishness and cold oblivious cares.
Among the farms and solitary huts,
Hamlets and thinly-scattered villages,
Where'er the aged Beggar takes his rounds,
The mild necessity of use compels
To acts of love ; and habit does the work
Of reason ; yet prepares that after-joy
Which reason cherishes. And thus the soul,
By that sweet taste of pleasure unpursued,
Doth find herself insensibly disposed
To virtue and true goodness.

To hard economic reasoners Wordsworth thus speaks :

But deem not this Man useless.—Statesmen ! ye
Who are so restless in your wisdom, ye
Who have a broom still ready in your hands
To rid the world of nuisances ; ye proud,
Heart-swoln, while in your pride ye contemplate
Your talents, power, or wisdom, deem him not
A burthen of the earth !

    .   .   .   .

May never HOUSE, misnamed of INDUSTRY,
Make him a captive !—for that pent-up din,
Those life-consuming sounds that clog the air,
Be his the natural silence of old age.

For years the misfortunes of the poor increased, while the fortunes of the rich multiplied. But before the close of the Napoleonic wars, which had contributed greatly to this one-sided prosperity, all agriculture entered a decline. In 1812 prices began to fall and by 1816 agricultural distress had become general.[9] The landlord and great farmer found themselves in the same boat with the small farmer and laborer. Now all classes on the land were experiencing hardship.

With the collapse of agriculture at the end of the Napoleonic wars,[1] many things closely associated with the agricultural revolution disappear from the scene. The *Annals of Agriculture* ceased publication in 1815. The Board of Agriculture, organized with such enthusiasm in 1793, began to decline in 1813, and in 1822 it became defunct.[2] The last of those great sheepshearing festivals begun at Holkham in 1778 was held

9. Curtler, pp. 244 ff.   1. See Hammond, pp. 151 ff.
2. Curtler, pp. 232-3.

in 1821. It was a magnificent occasion, but it was the last occasion. By 1820 this great agricultural movement originating in the eighteenth century had run its course. That year saw the death of Arthur Young, then blind, whose life and work had covered almost exactly this agricultural period. Spring had gone, and summer and autumn too. Winter is come, and now we hear the lamentations of the mourner William Cobbett.

Cobbett's *Rural Rides* (1821–32) are particularly interesting for the picture they give of English agriculture in this period of depression following the Napoleonic wars. During the third decade of the nineteenth century, Cobbett was riding regularly through the principal agricultural counties of England, especially the fertile southern counties which provided the food for that "great wen" of London. He was looking for a borough where he could stand for election to Commons—even a rotten one might do, though he is more than outspoken in his criticism of such boroughs where a handful of votes can send two men to the "collective wisdom" (Commons). Everywhere Cobbett meets in the countryside scenes to make his heart ache. If he goes to a country fair in 1822, he sees fine horses and cattle being sold for one-third the price they fetched ten years ago in the boom period.[3] Fields which were cultivated in the better years lie fallow, overgrown with thistles.[4] Agricultural societies can no longer afford to offer premiums for improvements.[5] Hardest hit of all in this depression is the laborer, whose wages Cobbett finds are as low as six shillings a week, with no supplement from the garden or cow or pig which the commons formerly supported.[6] "Their dwellings are little better than pig-beds, and their looks indicate that their food is not nearly equal to that of a pig."[7] Laborer, farmer, and landlord alike are involved in an economic catastrophe.

Groups of farmers, as many as three to five hundred, would gather at inns, such as the Swan Inn at Winchester, to hear Cobbett explain in one of his "rustic harangues" the cause of this agricultural depression. The government, he told them, was paying back to the "stock-jobbers and Jews" of London the money borrowed for the execution of the war against Napoleon. This debt was being met by taxing the land. To Cobbett it seemed that the Napoleonic wars were a conspiracy on the part of the banking interests of London to bleed the soil of its wealth. The new mansions of these enriched city jobbers could be seen lining the road for miles outside London.[8] To prevent a repetition of this injustice perpetrated against the country by the city, Cobbett's remedy was to be a reformed parliament, which ironically enough was just the reform which was to enthrone finally the bourgeois power.

But the fortunes of the landed interests were to be overshadowed by

3. *Rural Rides*, 1, 93.   4. *Idem*, 1, 114.   5. *Idem*, 1, 10.
6. *Idem*, 1, 116.   7. *Idem*, 1, 18.   8. *Idem*, 1, 65.

something more lasting than a temporary economic depression. By 1820 England, no longer rural, was about to enter that industrial age, interpreted by Carlyle, when the captains of agriculture were displaced by the captains of industry, the Plugsons of Undershot. These greater economic circumstances were to make England's prominent country classes fit subject for elegy, even as the poor peasant had been in times gone by.

II

Agrarian Economists: The Physiocrats and Adam Smith

IN the principal economic writings of the later eighteenth century, both in England and in France, we find a body of opinion that in many ways favored agriculture and a rural life. Voltaire remarks: "Vers 1750 la nation rassasiée de vers, de tragédies, de comédies, d'opéras, de romans, d'histoires romanesques, de réflexions morales plus romanesques encore, et de disputes théologiques sur la grâce et sur les convulsions, se mit à raisonner sur les blés."[1] Grimm made a similar observation upon the French scene in this same period. "La folie de l'agriculture, ayant succédé à la folie de la géométrie, qui de son côté avait succédé à la folie du bel esprit, les livres qui paraissent tous les jours sur cette matière sont innombrables."[2] These witticisms must glance chiefly at the writings of the physiocrats, who are sometimes spoken of as the first modern economists. In England, where so much was being done at this time in the improvement of the methods of agriculture, there was no agrarian school comparable to the physiocrats. But Adam Smith's *Wealth of Nations,* published in 1776, expressed a definite agrarian attitude which might almost be said to have been established into a school. The agrarian thoughts of the physiocrats and those of Adam Smith were, to be sure, quite different things. It will be worth while to separate these two strains of ruralism, which have some superficial and quite deceptive resemblance to each other.

The physiocrats do not seem to have been very close to the practical world of agriculture. Their associations were not so much with the country as with the court of Versailles and the Parisian salon of Mme de Marchai.[3] Perhaps they deserved the title they disavowed, "cultivateurs de cabinet."[4] Arthur Young, who regarded himself and all Englishmen as practical, was so contemptuous of the theoretical writing of the physiocrats as to call it "rubbish." But the physiocrats did understand money and profits even if they did not know much about the newest English ways of farming. As a group they have been described as *noblesse de robe,* gentlemen whose families had acquired fortunes from the bureaucracy of the French monarchy since the days of Louis xiv.[5] This capital they had invested in farm lands which an older nobility would

1. See Weulersse, I, 25. 2. *Idem,* II, 152.
3. *Idem,* I, 216–17. 4. *Idem,* II, 163.
5. See Norman J. Ware, "The Physiocrats," *American Economic Review,* XXI (1931), 607–19.

relinquish for cash. Possessing these wide acres and at the same time having a certain bourgeois background, these new landowners wished to make the most of their investments by improving the position of agriculture in the national economy of their country.

The principles of physiocracy were first clearly stated in Quesnay's *Tableau œconomique,* printed by the author himself on a private press at Versailles in 1758, with Louis xv helping set the type.[6] Mirabeau ranked the *Tableau œconomique* among the three great inventions of civilization, along with writing and money.[7] Whoever will study this remarkable table[8] will see that wealth originates in agriculture. The farmer produces not only food enough to support himself but also a surplus, which is wealth. This surplus of food supports the "sterile class" which includes principally the administrators of farm land and the artisans who in city manufacturing spend their time improving products of agriculture through weaving, dyeing, turning, and distilling. The teaching of the *Tableau œconomique* and its author is that the agricultural surplus is the sole source of national wealth, wherefore a nation's first interest must be its agriculture. A proper understanding of the importance of agriculture in the creation of national prosperity seemed to the early advocates of physiocracy to belong only to the much-admired Chinese.[9]

A prosperous national agriculture the physiocrats thought depended upon liberty. And this law for economic life they called a natural law. Like every other movement of the eighteenth century which would make itself respectable, the progressive laissez faire agricultural program of the physiocrats took nature on its side.[1] Quesnay, the father of this school, was a philosopher before he began to entertain his associates with economic tables in his surgeon's offices in the king's palace in Versailles. He was in particular a natural philosopher, a student of medicine, who had written an important book on the physiology of the human body. In the free circulation of the blood Quesnay saw the principle of natural liberty which he was to establish as the law for economic society. His analogy Adam Smith chose to repeat in arguing for a laissez faire economy in the *Wealth of Nations.*[2] Freedom for French agriculture would mean many things. There would still be taxes, but in place of a

6. Weulersse, I, 66.

7. V. de Mirabeau, *Philosophie rurale* (Amsterdam, 1764. 3 vols.), I, 44.

8. See *Tableau œconomique* (Facsimile ed. London, Macmillan, 1894).

9. See especially L. A. Maverick, "Chinese Influences upon the Physiocrats," *Economic History,* IV (1938), 54–67. See also Weulersse, I, 36, 76, 159. See also a review in *Gent. Mag.* XXXIX (1769), 494, 591, of M. le Poivre's *Les Voyages d'un philosophe* (1768).

1. In editing the *Physiocratie* (Leyden, 1768), Dupont de Nemours rounds out considerably Quesnay's rather bleak remarks about natural law. Dupont's hundred-page introductory discourse is an exposition of natural law—the natural law which has made agriculture the foundation of economic life, the natural law which confers property upon men, the natural law which forbids interference with the processes of the economic order.

2. *Wealth of Nations,* II, 186–7. See Gide and Rist, pp. 7–8, 18.

multiple tax system of which tithes were a part, there would be a single and smaller land tax. Furthermore, in a system of freedom, agricultural products might move from province to province, from country to city, without being taxed at every turn. The limitations upon the market which since the days of Colbert had worked against agriculture in favor of industry would be removed, and country products would be free to find their best market, whether that market were domestic or foreign. Such freedoms would make for greater profits in agriculture: these profits in turn would be used in improving land and stock upon English patterns, to the greater increase of the agricultural surplus, or national wealth.

Liberty in the language of physiocracy had, we may note, a quite restricted meaning. The physiocrats were not advocates of political liberty or social equality. Accepting a system of monarchy and classes, they did not extend the principle of freedom beyond the economic sphere. Though they perhaps provided the economic theory for the French Revolution,[3] it is surely quite wrong to interpret their position as wholly revolutionary, as some have done, including Coleridge, who wrote:

At the commencement of the French Revolution, in the remotest villages every tongue was employed in echoing and enforcing the almost geometrical abstractions of the physiocratic politicians and economists. The public roads were crowded with armed enthusiasts disputing on the inalienable sovereignty of the people, the imprescriptible laws of the pure reason, and the universal constitution, which as rising out of the nature and rights of man as man, all nations alike were under the obligation of adopting.[4]

Liberty in a rather limited form was the first requisite of an agriculture that was to be the basis of national prosperity. The second demand of physiocracy was that agriculture be conducted on a large scale by rich farmers. Only great cultivators were able to farm in such a way as to produce that surplus of food and farm products which is wealth; only great cultivators could employ the improved methods of agriculture, which demanded that one drain, fertilize, mechanize; only rich farmers could farm with the horse, symbol of the *grande agriculture*. The physiocrats envisioned a France of rich proprietors and cultivators, farming the soil in the most up-to-date English style. They never entertained the humble dream of a France of little country cottages, occupied by simple farmers who owned their small lands and worked them in the old way, producing enough for themselves but little *produit net* to support the other classes of society. For this type of farming they had nothing but contempt. Quesnay's fifteenth maxim in the *Physiocratie* reads:

3. Gide and Rist, p. 104.
4. *The Statesman's Manual* (1816), quoted in *The Poetical Works of William Wordsworth*, W. Knight, ed. (Edinburgh, W. Paterson, 1882–89. 11 vols.), v, 136 n.

Que les terres employées à la culture des grains soient réunies, autant qu'il est possible, en grandes fermes exploitées par de riches laboureurs; car il y a moins de dépense pour l'entretien & la réparation des bâtimens, & à proportion beaucoup moins de frais, & beaucoup plus de produit net dans les grandes entreprises d'agriculture, que dans les petites. La multiplicité de petits fermiers est préjudiciable à la population. La population la plus assurée, la plus disponible pour les différentes occupations & pour les différents travaux qui partagent les hommes en différentes classes, est celle qui est entretenue par le produit net. Toute épargne faite à profit dans les travaux qui peuvent s'exécuter par le moyen des animaux, des machines, de rivieres, &c. revient à l'avantage de la population de l'État, parceque plus de produit net procure plus de gain aux hommes pour d'autres services ou d'autres travaux.[5]

From this and from the other maxims, which are perhaps the best and most concise statement of the tenets of physiocracy, one sees that Quesnay was interested solely in the great proprietor who would be able to farm in a large and profitable way. "Pauvres paysans, pauvre royaume; pauvre royaume: pauvre roi." Mirabeau, though a better friend of man than Quesnay, endorsed, as did all physiocrats, the large-scale type of agriculture. The inhabitants of cities, he said, have decided in favor of small farms,

. . . parce qu'ils occuperoient un plus grand nombre d'hommes, & entretiendroient une plus grande population, & par conséquent une plus grande abondance de productions, qui seroient à bas prix par la concurrence de ces Paysans, forcés de vendre pour payer les impôts dont ils sont chargés, & qui est lui-même un aiguillon pour les forcer au travail; c'est ainsi que le Citadin croit avoir ses esclaves continuellement sous le joug, dans l'oppression & dans la misere; mais il seroit bien puni de cette abominable barbarie, si son sort dépendoit réellement de cet absurde système d'Agriculture, fondé sur la multitude d'hommes, employés au travail de la terre.[6]

En un mot, les gros Fermiers sont l'ame de l'Agriculture, la bénédiction de la Société, le salut, la richesse, la force & la puissance des Nations agricoles.[7]

What would happen to the small cultivator and laborer when farming was done on such a large scale with the aid of machines and with the minimum use of men? This population, released from agriculture, would give itself to other occupations, "d'autres travaux," which I take to mean industrial labor.

Physiocracy was an upper-class agrarian movement, but it had a popular significance not to be overlooked. This, indeed, was necessary in the case of men of the quality of Mirabeau and Dupont, for their hearts were as much at stake in this world as their fortunes. The popular worth of physiocracy was to be found in its benefits to population. Ques-

5. *Physiocratie*, pp. 114–15.   6. *Philosophie rurale*, ii, 220.
7. *Idem*, ii, 224. See Weulersse, i, 334 ff.

nay mentions the argument frequently: the greater surplus of food you produce, the more people you may feed.[8] Mirabeau's primary social interest had been the increasing of population,[9] which would in turn develop the lands of France. He was persuaded by Quesnay that the process should be reversed: a prosperous agriculture would increase population. Physiocracy was presented to him as a system of agriculture, capitalistic as it was, which would produce to the profit of great cultivators an enormous surplus supporting a tremendous population employed in activities other than agriculture. In this way the "friend of man" could find happiness in physiocratic schemes as well as in seeing a wealthy upper class to which he belonged returning to their lands to lead virtuous lives in active supervision of their estates. These were goods, though it required shutting one's eyes to the fact that a vast part of the population would be condemned to industry. "Men multiply like rats in a barn, if they have the means of subsistence," writes Mirabeau. "The means of subsistence are the measure of population."[1] Mirabeau regarded physiocracy as accordant with Christ's teaching, that we feed the hungry and clothe the naked.[2] It conformed also to the command: increase and multiply.[3] Malthus, who praised the interest of the physiocrats in population and indeed accepted their fundamental position, thought England represented the populous state envisioned by physiocracy.

Her system of agriculture is beyond comparison better, and consequently her surplus produce is more considerable. France is very greatly superior to England in extent of territory and population; but when the surplus produce, or disposeable revenue of the two nations are compared, the superiority of France almost vanishes. And it is this great surplus produce in England, arising from her agriculture, which enables her to support such a vast body of manufactures, such formidable fleets and armies, such a crowd of persons engaged in the liberal professions, and a proportion of the society living on money rents, very far beyond what has ever been known in any other country of the world.[4]

While physiocracy had its popular side, it was in no way a democratic agrarian movement, for its rural society was to be centered not in the peasant but in the gentleman farmer. The class associations of physiocracy are particularly evident in the literature it inspired. Addressed as it was to gentlemen, this literature held up the image, not of the simple peasant but of the splendid gentleman farmer. Voltaire, who believed in cultivating gardens, also believed in cultivating farms. Having made something of a failure in business enterprises,[5] he had turned to farm-

8. *Physiocratie*, pp. 158 ff.   9. See Weulersse, I, 53 ff.
1. Quoted in Henry Higgs, *The Physiocrats* (London, Macmillan, 1897), p. 21.
2. *Philosophie rurale*, I, 153.   3. *Idem*, III, 73.
4. *Essay on the Principle of Population* (New ed., enlarged. London, 1803), pp. 437-8.
5. Weulersse, I, 197 ff.

ing, which he thought involved less financial risk. We are told that he was a practitioner of the new Tullian, or English, methods of agriculture.[6] But he was also a physiocrat who, though he ridiculed economic tables,[7] accepted the fundamental hypothesis that agriculture is the source of all national wealth. In a letter to Haller in 1759, he wrote: "Tout ce que nous avons de mieux à faire sur la terre, c'est de la cultiver; . . . Honneur à celui qui fertilise la terre; malheur au misérable, ou courronné, ou encasqué, ou tonsuré, qui la trouble!"[8] And his *Épitre sur l'agriculture* of 1761, appearing in the first years of physiocracy, was addressed exactly to those polite circles which were to be the center of a physiocratic order.[9]

> C'est la cour qu'on doit fuir, c'est aux champs
> qu'il faut vivre.
>
> .   .   .   .
>
> La Nature t'appelle, apprends à l'observer;
> La France a des déserts, ose les cultiver . . .
>
> .   .   .   .
>
> L'arbre qu'on a planté rit plus à notre vue
> Que le parc de Versaille et sa vaste étendue.

In November of 1765 there appeared in Paris a little paper, the *Éphémérides du citoyen, ou chronique de l'esprit national,*[1] edited by the Abbé Baudeau who thought he was giving to his country a paper like the *Spectator*. But whereas the *Spectator* had reflected a bourgeois spirit, the *Éphémérides* took as its chief purpose the promotion of the rural idea. Baudeau's attitude toward bourgeois industry is well shown in a version of biblical history given in two early issues of the *Éphémérides*.[2] The first crime of man, we are told, led to industry in the production of clothing, whence it follows that industry is, as one might expect, the issue of sin. Cain's posterity, the "sons of men," were a race given to luxury and the arts, who made much of dress and began work in metals. They invented architecture too, built houses and cities. The sons of Seth, the "sons of God," were on the contrary a simple pastoral people, whose lives were characterized by "la candeur & la médriocrité rustique." But the designing daughters of men, dressed up by the aid of their arts to appear attractive, seduced the sons of God, who foolishly preferred them to their shepherdesses, "des Bergeres, simples, robustes, peut-être grossieres, qui n'avoient que la vertu, le bon sens & les graces

6. *DNB,* under Jethro Tull.
7. *L'Homme aux quarante écus* (1768).
8. Quoted from Weulersse, I, 89, n. 2.
9. "Épitre à Madame Denis, sur l'agriculture," *Oeuvres complètes* (Paris, Garnier, 1877–85. 52 vols.), x, 378–82. See Weulersse, I, 89 ff.
1. For a bibliographical account of this magazine's complicated history, see *Dict. Pol. Econ.,* I, 743 ff.
2. February 24, 1766; April 21, 1766.

de la nature." The corrupt urban civilization which ensued was wiped out by the Flood, and humanity was preserved alone through Noah, who was "Agricole." But Noah's posterity in days after the Flood did not observe the simplicity of manners that had characterized the rural Noah and the families of Seth. "Les charmes de la vie pastorale furent presque oubliés . . ." Simple shepherds began appearing on feast days in "voiles brodés & . . . tuniques brillantes," and civilization was again well on its way to the urbanity and luxury sought by the sons of men.

Baudeau's rural evangelism, we come shortly to see, was directed principally toward the nobility and upper classes of France who had shown no proper appreciation of rural life since the days of Henry IV and Sully. The nobility, he tells us in the third issue of *Éphémérides*,[3] used to spend the major part of the autumn in the country, far away from the city. For them this was "un tems destiné au soin de sa santé, au goût des plaisirs les plus simples & les plus touchants, à la pratique des vertus les plus douces & les plus utiles à la société . . ." They lived in simple "maisons de champs," and in all ways they lived simply.

Dans ces retraites embellies des charmes les plus naturels, on reprenoit des moeurs aussi simples & aussi pures que l'air qu'on y respiroit. Jaloux de profi- ter des avantages de la saison, tout le monde se levoit avec le jour : on oublioit le soin importun de la parure, pour ne s'occuper que du plus merveilleux de tous les spectacles, des roses dont l'aurore peint le ciel, & des perles dont elle abreuve la terre, de la vigueur que le retour du soleil paroit ranimer dans toute la nature, & des hommages que les oiseaux rendent par leurs concerts à ses premiers rayons. Un déjeuner frugal, assaisonné par l'appétit, étoit la suite d'une douce rêverie, & réparoit la fatigue légere d'une matinée délicieuse.

Such customs have passed. Now, when our upper classes do go to the country, they carry along into the villages "tout l'attirail du luxe, tous les poisons de la sensualité, tous les rafinements de l'indolence, tous les travers enfin, toutes les erreurs & toutes les passions des grandes Villes." Their residences in the country are now "vastes & superbes palais," sur- rounded with artificial gardens, "de longs portiques de fer & de bois enluminés, d'une verdure artificielle, & d'ombre sans feuillage." In these luxurious surroundings they set about to restore constitutions ruined by the dissipations of the city. Sleeping away the entire morning, they rise late to fortify themselves with the brews of America and Asia, coffee and tea. If one takes fifty steps down a shaded arbor, protected with mantle and parasol, it is a grand and rare effort of courage. The entire afternoon is spent in the consumption of one enormous meal, after which one might take a short walk, counting the steps, or a ride in a coach with the windows carefully closed. The evening is spent with music and dancing which sometimes last well on into the night, even

3. November 11, 1765.

to the light. "Le Soleil est déja levé, & la campagne pleine de ses vrais Habitans, quand on se retire pour se livrer au someil." Elegant urbanity, which brings to the country all the pleasures of the city, takes no interest in the improvement of land or the welfare of the humble cultivators, and the landlord is no longer regarded by the people of the hamlet as their father, their protector, their resource. He is unknown to those who work his lands, and his first care is often to take down all their dwellings in the environs of his palace to make room for *allées* and parks, to stock the lands with a million animals for hunting. A hundred cultivators are dismissed to make way for these pleasures.

Roman history, and classical culture generally, offered Baudeau suitable examples of nobility associated with the greatest rural simplicity.[4] Roman consuls, after serving their terms of office, returned to the land to preside over their inheritances. When in a moment of national danger the Republic made one of its greatest generals dictator, it was necessary to seek him in the plowed fields. Ambassadors from conquered kings, loaded with bribes, met the refusal of such a victor, whom they would find in his humble country retreat preparing a frugal meal of the roots he had himself planted and dug. But the nobility of France were for the most part living away from their lands in the city of Paris, indulging themselves in luxuries produced by an urban artisan class whose demoralization in the city was only less conspicuous than that of the noblesse.

Baudeau's intentions in thus addressing the gentlemen of France in his attractive little journal seem to have been purely moral. But his sentiments were generally so suitable to the purposes of the physiocrats that they adopted him—whereupon the *Éphémérides* began to print figures demonstrating that ruralism was the best policy, that the country lane led to wealth as well as to virtue.

In 1768 Parisian society was being entertained with a play by Favart, entitled *Les Moissonneurs,* which was quickly translated into a very lively English version with the title *The Reapers: or the Englishman out of Paris* (London, 1770). The hero Candor (or Allworthy in the English version) is a gentleman who for a year or so has known the joy of caring for his estate. "What a morning!—and—what a prospect!" he says as he looks out over the field at his reapers. In the figure of Candor we see the gentleman made perfect by living in the country. His calmness of spirit contrasts with the turbulence of his dissipated nephew, who comes down from the city intent on hunting game, even across fields of corn. Having a composed, classical mind, Candor is also a man of more modern benevolence, who sees that his reapers have ale to drink when hot, that they work in the shade when the sun is high. The plot of this play is a repetition of the eighteenth century's best pastoral story:

4. *Éphémérides,* November 15, 1765.

it tells of the marriage of this worthy country gentleman to an equally worthy young lady of quality who lives in cottage obscurity as a gleaner. This rather elegant rural drama was milk and honey to the physiocrats, who were said to have patronized the production.[5] Physiocrat Mirabeau, though a trifle disappointed because its maxims were not quite physiocratic enough, wrote to Rousseau, "Le public pleure sans cesse aux tableaux et aux peintures de la vie champêtre enluminée de bienfaisance et d'amour reconnaissant."[6] The *Journal d'agriculture* turned dramatic critic: "Candor, le principal personnage de la pièce, ne représente-t-il pas tous les grands et riches citoyens qui, secondant les vues du gouvernement, ne s'occupent que de faire fleurir l'agriculture et de relever l'état du cultivateur?"[7]

In these days of physiocracy the cultured gentleman straying in Paris was receiving many an engraved invitation to return to the country to a life that would be good both for himself and for his country. The chief poet of physiocracy was probably Saint-Lambert, whose *Saisons* of 1769 embodies all the standard physiocratic objectives, such as free trade,[8] the introduction of progressive English agricultural methods,[9] and large-scale farming. Saint-Lambert, as we might expect, addresses his rural poetry only to the noblesse and rich citizens. In fact he thinks of himself as the first poet to celebrate the delights that may be enjoyed by the noblesse in the country. "Il y a un ordre d'hommes dont les Poëtes champêtres n'ont jamais parlé: ce sont les Nobles . . ."[1] Speaking of the moral of his poem he says:

Je n'ai point perdu de vue le dessein d'inspirer à la Noblesse & aux Citoyens riches, l'amour de la campagne & le respect pour la vie champêtre.

Il est utile, sur-tout dans ce moment, d'inspirer aux premières classes des citoyens le goût de la vie champêtre.

Peut-être la Noblesse pensera-t-elle enfin, que dans les moments où elle n'est pas nécessaire à nos Armées, elle peut employer son tems à éclairer ses vassaux, à perfectionner l'Agriculture & à s'enrichir par des moyens qui enrichissent l'Etat.[2]

Saint-Lambert dispenses with the peasant in these physiocratic words: "Il n'y faut pas placer [dans les paysages] de malheureux paysans; ils n'intéressent que par leurs malheurs; ils n'ont pas plus de sentiments que d'idées; leurs moeurs ne sont pas pures; la nécessité les force à tromper . . ."[3]

In October, 1770, the *Gentleman's Magazine* reviewed a French novel

5. Weulersse, I, 166. 6. *Idem*, II, 153.
7. Quoted in *idem*, II, 153-4.
8. *Les Saisons* (Amsterdam, 1769), pp. 162 ff.
9. *Idem*, pp. 110 ff. 1. *Idem*, p. xxi.
2. *Idem*, pp. xxv–xxvii. 3. *Idem*, pp. xx–xxi.

entitled *La Jolie femme, ou la femme du jour,* published at Lyons the previous year.[4] An episode which the reviewer singles out as among the best describes a gentleman, Sainval, who, having tired of the luxurious circles of bon ton, had come to reside at his estate and employ himself in agriculture. ". . . After the example of our masters, the wise English," he practices improved methods of farming. For example, he cuts his grain close to the ear so it is not injured in falling. His old city friends, when they come to visit, are shocked to see "his spacious coach houses . . . filled with all the implements of rural economy." Statues, arbors, orange trees, and all efforts of art have been removed from the garden. "Surely we are in a farm," exclaims Madame de Lorevel. ". . . Heavens! a kitchen garden in a parterre!" His friends depart in boredom and disgust to spread the word everywhere that "Sainval was become a fool, unpolite, self-opinionated, whimsical, a Farmer, and, in short, a Philosopher." In Sainval we may see a French version of the progressive English farmer, but we also recognize in him the physiocrat, for his favorite book is Mirabeau's *Friend of Man.* He is a good image of that country gentleman who was central to the economic scheme of the physiocrats.

The Rook

When we turn from the work of the French physiocrats to Adam Smith's *Wealth of Nations,* which appeared in 1776, we see again in economic writing the expression of a strong agrarian feeling, some of which may be derived from the physiocrats themselves, whose doctrines Adam Smith learned at first hand during his sojourn in France in the

4. XL, 456–7.

years 1764 to 1766.[5] With much of their thought he was in sympathy. He felt the fundamental importance of agriculture. While he does not assert that agriculture alone is productive and industry sterile, he does often declare in the course of the *Wealth of Nations* that agriculture is superior to industry in its productivity,[6] that the greatest improvements in society result from the development of agriculture.[7] The wisdom of China in preferring agriculture above industry was, like other aspects of Chinese wisdom, apparent to this eighteenth-century Scot. With the physiocrats' major tenet Adam Smith agreed. "Nothing can be more incorrect, though it is frequently done, than to regard Smith as the prophet of industrialism and to contrast him with the Physiocrats, the champions of agriculture." He "clung to agriculture with all the tenacity of his nature, and no opportunity of showing his preference was ever missed."[8] But Adam Smith differed widely from the physiocrats on the significant issue of the scale upon which agriculture should be conducted.

Who reads the *Wealth of Nations* aright will recognize that there runs throughout an attack upon bigness—bigness in all forms, big industry, big universities, big nations, and, no less, big agriculture. It is difficult for the contemporary reader of the *Wealth of Nations* to visualize the small units in which Adam Smith believed that the work of the world should be accomplished. His world would have been one of little properties, a world of great equality. The *raison d'être* of this economy was established in moral philosophy, of which Adam Smith was a lifelong student. The earlier Adam Smith, who was much attracted to Rousseau and who wrote so vividly of sympathy in the *Theory of Moral Sentiments,* exhibited some tendency toward sentimentality. But as he grew older, perhaps because of narrowing his interest more closely to the economic

5. John Rae, *Life of Adam Smith* (London, Macmillan, 1895), pp. 174 ff.
6. *Wealth of Nations,* I, 368; II, 259.
7. *Idem,* I, 370. See also *Lectures* . . . *Glasgow,* p. 224.
8. Gide and Rist, pp. 65, 67. See W. R. Scott, *Adam Smith* (London, Oxford University Press, n.d.), pp. 18 ff. (from *Proceedings of the British Academy,* XI). See Smith's important account of the physiocrats in the last chapter of Book IV of the *Wealth of Nations.* Here is an instance that suggests the borrowing of lesser things from their writings. In the *Éphémérides* (December 6, 1765), Baudeau, in speaking of the demoralizing aspects of a luxurious life in the city, has said: "Des femmes plus accablées encore des chaînes de la mollesse voluptueuse, leur produisent à peine un ou deux avortons de l'espece humaine, que le moindre souffle détruit long-tems avant le moment de leur maturité." The striking resemblance of this sentence to a passage in Adam Smith has not been noted.

"Poverty [he writes in the first book of the *Wealth of Nations*], though it no doubt discourages, does not always prevent marriage. It seems even to be favourable to generation. A half-starved Highland woman frequently bears more than twenty children, while a pampered fine lady is often incapable of bearing any, and is generally exhausted by two or three. Barrenness, so frequent among women of fashion, is very rare among those of inferior station. Luxury in the fair sex, while it inflames perhaps the passion for enjoyment, seems always to weaken, and frequently to destroy altogether, the powers of generation." *Wealth of Nations,* I, 83.

world, he became more cognizant of the selfishness of men.[9] This change of ethical views is discussed by the German critics as *Das Adam Smith Problem*. In his earlier *Glasgow Lectures* Adam Smith suggests that benevolence has some part in supplying the world's commodities.[1] However, by the time of the *Wealth of Nations,* he has no doubt that it is the single, unlovely principle of self-interest that prompts barter and exchange. In a famous sentence, he now declares: "It is not from the benevolence of the butcher, the brewer, or the baker, that we expect our dinner, but from their regard to their own interest."[2] But the realism of the eighteenth century, unlike the realism of other ages, was tempered by an optimism which, if it made men a little foolish, also saved them from despair. The optimistic philosopher, believing that all is for the best in this best of all possible worlds, holds that the all-wise and benevolent God who made this world can admit no partial evil which is not necessary for the universal good. So Adam Smith, an optimist, recognized that the self-interest in man's nature which, narrowly considered, would be regarded as bad, when left to work itself out naturally in society, would result in a social good. Thus in trade, an ugly self-interest would prompt a man to supply a very inferior product at a very high price. But the "invisible hand," which Adam Smith remembers in the *Wealth of Nations,*[3] has prepared a corrective for the self-interest of one man, which is competition, or the self-interest of another. A man, trying to sell his products in a free market in human society, because of competition with others is obliged to turn out a product superior if possible to that of rivals, and at a cheaper price. The neatness of this trick of Divine Providence left the eighteenth-century deist aghast![4]

Adam Smith wanted an economic world which was in the highest sense "natural"—a society which had in it the most of these principles of self-interest and competition which God in his inscrutable wisdom had seen fit to create at some unbiblical date as the twin poles between which man's economic life was to be held in perfect balance. Obvious it is that that individual has the strongest self-interest in his occupation whom necessity compels to work. He works the hardest who needs to. If a man's livelihood is secured through some privilege, he will not extend himself. The Church of England and the universities of Oxford

9. But see Glenn R. Morrow, "Adam Smith: Moralist and Philosopher," *Adam Smith, 1776-1926* (Chicago, University of Chicago Press, 1928), p. 166.
1. "Besides, it is by the wisdom and probity of those with whom we live that a propriety of conduct is pointed out to us, and the proper means of attaining it. Their valour defends us, their benevolence supplies us, the hungry is fed, the naked is clothed, by the exertion of these divine qualities." *Lectures . . . Glasgow,* p. 160.
2. *Wealth of Nations,* I, 15.
3. *Idem,* II, 28.
4. Cf. Wordsworth, *Prose Works,* I, 159: "Wicked actions indeed have oftentimes happy issues: the benevolent œconomy of nature counter-working and diverting evil; and educing finally benefits from injuries, and turning curses to blessings."

and Cambridge were for Adam Smith splendid examples of lethargy, for the very reason that they were privileged institutions with assured incomes. "In the University of Oxford, the greater part of the public professors have for these many years given up altogether even the pretence of teaching."[5] Smith says that in his century those subjects best taught were fencing, dancing, riding, and the spoken languages, because the teachers were individual freelance instructors, whose livelihood depended upon their own efforts.[6] The active ministers of the eighteenth century were those of new or poor sects (Methodists, he has in mind), that possessed no means but such as their efforts and striving could create.[7] Adam Smith argued that self-interest was most pronounced in a society where men, without the security of privilege or wealth, were working to make their living. Similarly, competition, which is the second natural law correcting the evils of self-interest, was most abundant in a society where the units of production were most numerous, where there were the most competitors. The natural economic order, then, was clearly one of numerous small producers, where each was working actively for his livelihood in keenest rivalry with his fellows.

Such an order Adam Smith visualized for the business world, for education, for religion, and likewise for agriculture. Unlike the physiocrats, he thought small farming more productive than large-scale agriculture. Having explained the circumstances in feudal life which made it necessary, for the sake of security, that lands be held in large units, he says:

Great tracts of uncultivated land were, in this manner, not only engrossed by particular families, but the possibility of their being divided again was as much as possible precluded for ever. It seldom happens, however, that a great proprietor is a great improver. In the disorderly times which gave birth to those barbarous institutions, the great proprietor was sufficiently employed in defending his own territories, or in extending his jurisdiction and authority over those of his neighbours. He had no leisure to attend to the cultivation and improvement of land. When the establishment of law and order afforded him this leisure, he often wanted the inclination, and almost always the requisite abilities. If the expense of his house and person either equalled or exceeded his revenue, as it did very frequently, he had no stock to employ in this manner. If he was an economist, he generally found it more profitable to employ his annual savings in new purchases than in the improvement of his old estate. To improve land with profit, like all other commercial projects, requires an exact attention to small savings and small gains, of which a man born to a great fortune, even though naturally frugal, is very seldom capable. The situation of such a person naturally disposes him to attend rather to ornament which pleases his fancy, than to profit for which he has so little occasion.[8]

5. *Wealth of Nations*, II, 346.   6. *Idem*, II, 350.
7. *Idem*, II, 372-4.   8. *Idem*, I, 389.

The wealth of the large landholder eliminates his desire to cultivate his land with the same thoroughness which the small possessor is required for his very livelihood to employ. At the other economic extreme, the slave has not the self-interest in the improvement of land that the freeman has, for his rewards can never be in any proportion to his efforts. Whatever work the slave does beyond what is necessary for his own maintenance can be squeezed out of him by violence only.[9] The best improver of the soil, Smith asserts, is the small proprietor.

A small proprietor, . . . who knows every part of his little territory, who views it with all the affection which property, especially small property, naturally inspires, and who upon that account takes pleasure not only in cultivating but in adorning it, is generally of all improvers the most industrious, the most intelligent, and the most successful.[1]

Devoted as he was to small proprietorship, Adam Smith opposed primogeniture and entail, as these laws kept land in the hands of the few. Against these outworn institutions of the Middle Ages, useful in their day, he argued with all the energy of a radical seeking a redistribution of property. Entail, which prevented the sale of land and the break-up of large estates, he regarded as a ridiculous extension of the property rights of the testator. These laws of primogeniture and entail, he said, "are founded upon the most absurd of all suppositions, the supposition that every successive generation of men have not an equal right to the earth, and to all that it possesses . . ."[2]

We have seen how the image of the gentleman farmer dominated physiocracy and the literature associated with it. It is quite fitting that in the *Wealth of Nations*, which favors a more humble agrarian society, there is almost continuous praise of the peasant. Adam Smith did, it is true, regard with some affection the landlords of England. It was part of his rural credo that this class was not so subject as merchants and manufacturers to "the wretched spirit of monopoly."[3] He accordingly supposed that the landed interests of England would be receptive to his liberal ideas which were directed toward the wealth not of one class, or one nation, but of all nations.[4] But the persistent agrarian image in the *Wealth of Nations* is not the leisurely country gentleman but the peasant, the dirt farmer, the man who makes his living on the soil with the labor of his own hands. Thinking in values other than those of profit and loss, Adam Smith interprets fully the virtues of peasant life as he compares this type not, to be sure, with the gentleman farmer but with his fellow laborer in manufacturing.

9. See *idem*, I, 390 ff., for the effect of slave labor in agriculture. See also *Lectures* . . . *Glasgow*, p. 225.
1. *Wealth of Nations*, I, 418–19; see also I, 390.
2. *Idem*, I, 388.   3. *Idem*, II, 34–5.
4. *Idem*, I, xxxvi.

Both in knowledge and intelligence Smith supposed that the country laborer was the superior of the factory worker. In the *Wealth of Nations* we read:

No apprenticeship has ever been thought necessary to qualify for husbandry, the great trade of the country. After what are called the fine arts and the liberal professions, however, there is perhaps no trade which requires so great a variety of knowledge and experience. The innumerable volumes which have been written upon it in all languages may satisfy us that among the wisest and most learned nations, it has never been regarded as a matter very easily understood. And from all those volumes we shall in vain attempt to collect that knowledge of its various and complicated operations, which is commonly possessed even by the common farmer; how contemptuously soever the very contemptible authors of some of them may sometimes affect to speak of him. There is scarce any common mechanic trade, on the contrary, of which all the operations may not be as completely and distinctly explained in a pamphlet of a very few pages, as it is possible for words illustrated by figures to explain them. In the history of the arts, now publishing by the French Academy of Sciences, several of them are actually explained in this manner. The direction of operations besides, which must be varied with every change of the weather as well as with many other accidents, requires much more judgment and discretion than that of those which are always the same or very nearly the same.

Not only the art of the farmer, the general direction of the operations of husbandry, but many inferior branches of country labour require much more skill and experience than the greater part of mechanic trades. The man who works upon brass and iron, works with instruments and upon materials of which the temper is always the same, or very nearly the same. But the man who ploughs the ground with a team of horses or oxen, works with instruments of which the health, strength, and temper are very different upon different occasions. The condition of the materials which he works upon too is as variable as that of the instruments which he works with, and both require to be managed with much judgment and discretion. The common ploughman, though generally regarded as the pattern of stupidity and ignorance, is seldom defective in this judgment and discretion. He is less accustomed, indeed, to social intercourse than the mechanic who lives in a town. His voice and language are more uncouth and more difficult to be understood by those who are not used to them. His understanding, however, being accustomed to consider a greater variety of objects, is generally much superior to that of the other, whose whole attention from morning till night is commonly occupied in performing one or two very simple operations. How much the lower ranks of people in the country are really superior to those of the town, is well known to every man whom either business or curiosity has led to converse much with both. In China and Hindostan accordingly both the rank and the wages of country labourers are said to be superior to those of the greater part of artificers and manufacturers. They would probably be so everywhere, if corporation laws and the corporation spirit did not prevent it.[5]

5. *Idem*, I, 133–4.

In the latter part of this passage we find Adam Smith's special reason for asserting the intellectual superiority of the farmer over the mechanic. As a philosopher, he accepted Locke's *tabula rasa* interpretation of the human mind and held, like a good eighteenth-century sensationalist, that the understanding develops in proportion to the number of objects it must relate.[6] Eighteenth-century industry was being conducted more and more with a division of labor, which demanded that one man perform but a single operation, acquiring thereby proficiency and also saving the time lost in moving from one operation to another. In such a simple manufacture as that of making pins, the use of divided labor among ten men would cause a workman's productivity to increase, Smith figured, 240 times, or even possibly 4800 times.[7] Production was being increased tremendously by use of the division of labor, but at the same time the minds of the workers in such a system were being impaired because of the monotony of their occupation.

In the progress of the division of labour, the employment of the far greater part of those who live by labour, that is, of the great body of the people, comes to be confined to a few very simple operations; frequently to one or two. But the understandings of the greater part of men are necessarily formed by their ordinary employments. The man whose whole life is spent in performing a few simple operations, of which the effects too are, perhaps, always the same, or very nearly the same, has no occasion to exert his understanding or to exercise his invention in finding out expedients for removing difficulties which never occur. He naturally loses, therefore, the habit of such exertion, and generally becomes as stupid and ignorant as it is possible for a human creature to become. The torpor of his mind renders him not only incapable of relishing or bearing a part in any rational conversation, but of conceiving any generous, noble, or tender sentiment, and consequently of forming any just judgment concerning many even of the ordinary duties of private life.[8]

This stultifying process was beginning at the very earliest age for the thousands of children who at the age of four or five were being sold to the factories to perform some simple and monotonous operation on the machine that had made possible factory work for children.[9] In the fifth book of his *Wealth of Nations,* Adam Smith calls upon the state to heal these wounds of the industrial system through education, pro-

6. *Idem,* II, 367. Cf. "Where the division of labour is brought to perfection, every man has only a simple operation to perform; to this his whole attention is confined, and few ideas pass in his mind but what have an immediate connexion with it. When the mind is employed about a variety of objects, it is somehow expanded and enlarged . . ." *Lectures . . . Glasgow,* p. 255.

7. *Wealth of Nations,* I, 6–7.

8. *Idem,* II, 365. Ever fond of pointing out the sources of Adam Smith, Marx cites Adam Ferguson's *Essay on the History of Civil Society* (Edinburgh, 1767) as anticipating Smith's realization of the evils of divided labor. *Capital,* Frederick Engels, ed. (New York, Modern Library, n.d.), p. 389.

9. See Mantoux, pp. 420 ff.

posing for the worker's salvation a government-sponsored educational program that would teach each man, destined as he might be for industrial labor, to read, to write, and to do accounts. Through reading, he hoped, the workman might come to know religion and enter its avenues of thought and speculation.

In agriculture, Smith points out, there is little opportunity to make use of a system of divided labor.

The nature of agriculture, indeed, does not admit of so many subdivisions of labour, nor of so complete a separation of one business from another, as manufactures. It is impossible to separate so entirely the business of the grazier from that of the corn-farmer, as the trade of the carpenter is commonly separated from that of the smith. The spinner is almost always a distinct person from the weaver; but the ploughman, the harrower, the sower of the seed, and the reaper of the corn, are often the same. The occasions for those different sorts of labour returning with the different seasons of the year, it is impossible that one man should be constantly employed in any one of them. This impossibility of making so complete and entire a separation of all the different branches of labour employed in agriculture, is perhaps the reason why the improvement of the productive powers of labour in this art does not always keep pace with their improvement in manufactures.[1]

The inability of agriculture to make use of divided labor preserves in rural work that versatility of occupation which accounts for the superior intelligence of the country laborer.

To morality, manufacturing and industry were as much a threat, Smith supposed, as they were to the intelligence. In the domestic system of industry a workman, employed in his own home or that of a neighbor, was not liable, he thought, to the temptations of bad company, as was the factory worker. Nor was the laborer in the village, on farm or in house, without particular persuasions toward goodness not felt in the city.

While he remains in a country village his conduct may be attended to, and he may be obliged to attend to it himself. In this situation, and in this situation only, he may have what is called a character to lose. But as soon as he comes into a great city, he is sunk in obscurity and darkness. His conduct is observed and attended to by nobody, and he is therefore very likely to neglect it himself, and to abandon himself to every sort of low profligacy and vice. He never emerges so effectually from this obscurity, his conduct never excites so much the attention of any respectable society, as by his becoming the member of a small religious sect. He from that moment acquires a degree of consideration which he never had before. All his brother sectaries are, for the credit of the sect, interested to observe his conduct, and if he gives occasion to any scandal, if he deviates very much from those austere morals which they almost always require of one another, to punish him by what is always a very severe

1. *Wealth of Nations*, I, 7–8.

punishment, even where no civil effects attend it, expulsion or excommunication from the sect.[2]

Though the morals of the worker in industry were improved by his association with religious societies, generally Methodist one may suppose, Adam Smith, deist that he was, took no pleasure in seeing the workman turning from the monotony of his factory work to the excitements of religious enthusiasm.

Adam Smith furthermore and finally supposed that the health of the country laborer was superior to that of the city worker, the artisan and the factory hand. In all forms of industry and manufacturing, he said, there is a considerable diminishing of the worker's strength. In some trades, where men work by the piece, the health of the worker is actually ruined by his excessive application to his trade. "A carpenter in London, and in some other places, is not supposed to last in his utmost vigour above eight years. . . . Almost every class of artificers is subject to some peculiar infirmity occasioned by excessive application to their peculiar species of work. Ramazzini, an eminent Italian physician, has written a particular book concerning such diseases."[3] In ancient Greece, Smith says,

. . . the employments of artificers and manufacturers were considered as hurtful to the strength and agility of the human body, as rendering it incapable of those habits which their military and gymnastic exercises endeavoured to form in it, and as thereby disqualifying it more or less for undergoing the fatigues and encountering the dangers of war.[4]

The agricultural laborer, by contrast, was robust and healthy, and for reason of his bodily strength as well as for the fact that the character of agricultural work resembled the activities of war, the farmer was prepared to take his part in war, which Adam Smith spoke of as the noblest of the arts.[5]

. . . among those nations of husbandmen who have little foreign commerce and no other manufactures but those coarse and household ones which almost every private family prepares for its own use, every man, in the same manner, either is a warrior, or easily becomes such. They who live by agriculture generally pass the whole day in the open air, exposed to all the inclemencies of the seasons. The hardiness of their ordinary life prepares them for the fatigues of war, to some of which their necessary occupations bear a great analogy. The necessary occupation of a ditcher prepares him to work in the trenches, and to fortify a camp as well as to enclose a field. The ordinary pastimes of such husbandmen are the same as those of shepherds, and are in the same manner the images of war. But as husbandmen have less leisure than shepherds, they are not so frequently employed in those pastimes. They are soldiers, but soldiers not quite so much masters of their exercise. Such as they

2. *Idem,* ii, 380.   3. *Idem,* i, 86.
4. *Idem,* ii, 268.   5. *Idem,* ii, 280.

are, however, it seldom costs the sovereign or commonwealth any expense to prepare them for the field.[6]

The agrarian ideal exhibited in the pages of the *Wealth of Nations* is something quite different from that which we discover in the work of the physiocrats. So far as England was concerned, both these schools of thought had a very living significance within the scene of the agricultural revolution.[7] While this agricultural revolution was driving the smaller classes from the land, the great improvers and enclosers justified the dispossession in the language of physiocracy. They believed that their program of improvement and enclosure would increase (as it did) the population of England, though that population would be located more and more in the cities. The physiocrat's population argument one will find echoed continually in the *Annals of Agriculture,* the organ of big agriculture in England. On the other hand, the cause of small farming in this period of decline was supported by the economic argument we find in the *Wealth of Nations,* that small farms were more productive. In Dr. Alexander Hunter's *Georgical Essays* (1803–4),[8] which show quite a democratic agrarian spirit by comparison with the physiocratic *Annals of Agriculture,*[9] edited by Arthur Young, we find essays arguing that small farms are more productive.[1] In his *Political Justice* Godwin argues also in the language of the *Wealth of Nations* in behalf of small rural properties. He asserts that in a system of equal ownership "the average cultivation of Europe might be so improved, as to maintain five

6. *Idem,* II, 276.

7. I suspect these ideas were also vital in America, in the conflict between the Federalists and the Jeffersonians. Federalism probably had a great deal of physiocracy in it. Washington wrote letters to the English *Annals of Agriculture* about the virtue and practice of agriculture (XXXVIII [1802], 306–16), and this journal spoke of him as a Cincinnatus (XVIII [1792], 162). Washington was an agrarian, but, I should suppose, in the manner of physiocracy, which envisioned a productive large-scale agriculture supplying an ever growing industrial urban population. Jefferson was also an agrarian, but however sympathetically he may have corresponded with the physiocrat Dupont, we may think of his agrarianism as following more in the pattern of Adam Smith's. See *The Correspondence of Jefferson and Du Pont de Nemours,* Gilbert Chinard, ed. (Baltimore, Johns Hopkins Press, 1931).

8. *Georgical Essays,* Alexander Hunter, ed. (York, 1803–4. 6 vols.).

9. *Annals.*

1. Nathaniel Kent, who was always on the liberal side, wrote for the *Georgical Essays* a paper "On the Size of Farms," advocating small farms of about £30 or £40 a year. He says: "It should . . . seem, even upon a slight consideration of the subject, that agriculture, when it is thrown into a number of hands, becomes the life of industry, the source of plenty, and the fountain of riches to a country; and that monopolized and grasped into a few hands, must dishearten the bulk of mankind . . ." v (1804), 280–6. In the same volume A. Dodsley wrote in an essay, "On Large and Small Farms," that 4,000 acres are better worked in 20 farms than as one. "The middling and low class of farmers are the most industrious, pains-taking people in the kingdom; they and their whole families toil incessantly . . ." So let us daily increase the number of small farmhouses and cottages, instead of reducing them. "Many thousands," he laments, "are gone abroad; many more, both men and women, have been driven from the country, and have exchanged a life of honest labour, for a vicious one of sloth and ease." *Idem,* pp. 405–18.

times her present number of inhabitants. . . . Thus the established administration of property, may be considered as strangling a considerable
portion of our children in their cradle."[2] Godwin cites among others
for his case Robert Wallace, author of *Various Prospects of Mankind,
Nature and Providence* (1761). Wallace's only hesitation, he says, in
endorsing a universal ownership of property is the fear that the earth
would become too fertile and in consequence dangerously overpopulated.[3]
Godwin prophesies a quintupling of the agriculture of Europe, when
the age of chivalry, which has made the great mass of mankind landless
slaves, is really dead. And Godwin, as one might guess, was attacked
in Young's progressive-conservative *Annals of Agriculture,* after the
appearance of *Political Justice.*[4]

In these days of the peasant's decline in England, many things were
said about the virtue of peasant life. The poetry of the period had high
arguments of its own in behalf of this disappearing class. But we may
find in literature of another order a testimony for the peasant very
similar to that made by Adam Smith—a testimony to the superior
intelligence, morality, and health to be found in this class. In the
Georgical Essays, which, as we have noted, seemed to favor a democratic
agrarian society, one meets many statements in praise of peasant virtue
and also of peasant health.[5] These volumes include an essay on the health

2. *Enquiry Concerning Political Justice* (3d ed. London, 1798. 2 vols.), II, 466-7.

3. *Idem,* II, 459 n. See Max Beer, *History of British Socialism* (London, G. Bell &
Sons, 1929. 2 vols.), I, 84.

4. Speaking of *Political Justice,* Young says free speech went too far with Tom Paine,
and now Godwin has gone further than Paine. "The object is palpable, and even avowed,
from the first page to the last of this bulky emanation of 'mind,'—LEVELLING PROPERTY."
". . . To level property, has long been the *real,* but it is now the *declared* object" of
Jacobinism. Godwin speaks openly of abolishing the rent roll of England, and talks of
" 'the right of the poor in the commonage of nature.' " Godwin is both atheistic and
immoral. This equalization of property, Young assures us, applies to property in woman.
Godwin means women should be held in common too, that the " 'rich may not deprive the
poor of the commonage of nature.' " *Annals,* XXI (1793), 175–85. W. Butts in the same
year and volume expresses similar disapproval. *Idem,* pp. 212–16. A conservative parable,
"The Land of Nineveh," appearing in the *Annals* in 1795, ends with the statement : "And
let property be held sacred, the sure basis of the prosperity of a state, AND ALL SHALL BE
WELL." *Idem,* XXIII (1795), 218–21.

5. In the *Georgical Essays* (1803) we find one paper entitled "On Agriculture and
Manufactures" and another "On the Beneficial Effects of a Spirited Agriculture." In the
former we read : "Agriculture, under due encouragement, will necessarily tend to a rapid
increase of population ; and by exciting in our youth a greater bias for the improvement
of land than for manufactures, it would render them more healthy, more attached to
their country, and therefore more to be depended on for its protection, than men can in
general be whose lives are usually spent in dissipation, as too frequently happens with
the lower class of manufacturers, when collected, as they now commonly are, in large
numbers together ; and who seldom place any value upon a country, but in proportion
to the money that they receive in it for their workmanship. Exceptions to this are, no
doubt, to be met with ; but it must be admitted, that a nation, whose youth consists mostly
of manufacturers, will never be so secure or independent, as it would be with the same
population employed in the cultivation of land." I, 275–6. The second of the essays speaks

of persons employed in agriculture,⁶ written by Dr. William Falconer, a well-known Bath physician and a strong agrarian spirit.⁷ Falconer observes in this essay that, while the agricultural laborer is subject to disorders resulting from overwork, overeating, and exposure, nevertheless, because of the variety of his work, his regular hours, and his diet of vegetables and milk, his health is much better than that of his fellow city worker. He breathes pure air, not tainted like that in cities, and he is not often exposed to the less salubrious night air. "The morning air, on the contrary, so celebrated both by poets and philosophers for its benign and cheering effects upon the mind and body, is enjoyed in high perfection by persons in this way of life: and the advantages they derive from thence in point of health are probably very great."⁸

---

thus of the virtue of country life: "And as Agriculture contributes to bodily health and vigour, so it tends to preserve innocency and simplicity of manners. At the same time that it promotes population, it obliges the people to continue in a divided and scattered state, thereby preventing that growth and prevalence of corruption, which an easy and frequent intercourse is so apt to produce. And as every day hath its particular task, which can seldom be anticipated or postponed, they have neither leisure nor opportunity allowed them for contracting habits of idleness and intemperance. By their situation and manner of life, they are prevented from being often witnesses to scenes of profligacy and vice, and thereby kept in a great measure free from the contagion of bad example; the frequency of which proves so destructive of the morals of the crowded city. Hard and constant labour serves to keep the passions in check, and affords no time for the contrivance and execution of deliberate schemes of wickedness." ii, 16–17.

6. iv (1803), 430–529.

7. In 1781 Falconer published a book which belongs very definitely to this agrarian age, a large quarto volume entitled *Remarks on the Influence of Climate, Situation, Nature of Country, Population, Nature of Food, and Way of Life, on the Disposition and Temper, Manners and Behaviour, Intellects, Laws and Customs, Form of Government, and Religion, of Mankind.* Four sections of this volume (Bk. vi, chaps. i–iv) consider the influence of savage, barbaric (pastoral), agricultural, and commercial states upon mankind. Falconer was no exponent of noble savagery and no disciple of Rousseau, who clung to the first period, though, as Mr. Lovejoy has shown, Rousseau's ideal world was not one of isolated hunters, a pure state of nature with man living alone, but a village life of hunting and fishing. Arthur Lovejoy, "The Supposed Primitivism of Rousseau's *Discourse on Inequality," Modern Philology,* xxi (1923–24), 165–86. Less attractive still than the savage state for Falconer was a barbaric state, or a true state of pastoralism. He does well to call our attention to the fact that the pastoralism so charmingly portrayed in literature belongs to a society which is basically agricultural. Real pastoral society is a state similar to that of the Tartars and Arabs, and according to Falconer it produced hard types. *Remarks . . . ,* p. 334. In his opinion, rural life exerts the most favorable influences upon mankind, and he sees many things in this life later observed and cherished by Wordsworth. He finds strong affection for home and country in rural society. One of the principal effects of agriculture, he tells us, is a character of settled disposition with a great degree of local attachment, in other words, a patriot. Moreover, among agricultural people he finds a greater respect for parents than in other cultures. "In the Greek republics, where agriculture was but little in esteem, the power of a father over his children was neither so great, or of so long duration, as in the Roman state." *Idem,* p. 373. His repeated example of the agricultural nation is Rome. But Falconer thinks that this ideal rural life is little favorable to works of fancy and genius, and he remarks that the Romans, who were agrarian, showed little taste for poetry till a late age, while the Greeks exhibited many marks of this genius. *Idem,* p. 378.

8. *Georgical Essays,* iv, 433.

Persons employed in daily labour of a healthy kind, and living on coarse food, naturally become robust and athletic, of a firm fibre, and dense blood. Hence inflammatory complaints are in such habits more common than those of the putrid kind; and such as are attended with low spirits and other hypochondriacal symptoms, are rarely met with. Evacuations may of course be used with more safety among such people, than among the effeminate inhabitants of populous towns.[9]

For England, then, these two traditions of agrarian thought, developed in economic writing, had a very living significance. Physiocratic thought was altogether suitable to the purposes of the improvers and enclosers; on the other hand, the humbler agrarian tradition, represented in the *Wealth of Nations,* cooperated with the spirit of poetry in behalf of England's declining peasantry.

9. *Idem,* IV, 467.

III

Wordsworth as Agrarian

IT may be pleasant to remember that Wordsworth's weakness for peasants was an acquired, not a natural, taste. His first poem, *An Evening Walk*, was a well-composed, polite piece of landscape painting, reflecting very nicely that delicate interest in sensations which we recognize as a mark of the late eighteenth-century mind. But there is little rusticity in the *Evening Walk*, and this little was in part removed in revision.[1] The *Descriptive Sketches*, based on his undergraduate ramble in the Alps, do contain a good deal about the peasants of these great mountains, but this material would seem to be rather conventional and bookish.[2] As he traveled in Switzerland he was interested less in people than in landscape, which was much too absorbing to leave him any time to insinuate himself into peasant cottages.[3] The Wordsworth of the French Revolution—that Wordsworth who after leaving the university lived for a while among the people of London, frequenting their pubs and places of amusement—the Wordsworth who went to France to learn the language and learned republican revolutionary theory instead—this Wordsworth was hardly interested in anything so mild as a peasant democracy. His mind was on larger things, on nothing smaller than a whole new world order. He must have been an impressive young man in those days: he was laying out leftwing journals; he was

---

1. In revising this poem Wordsworth omitted the following lines (ll. 117–18) which describe sheep feeding beside cross-shaped stone walls peculiar to the Lake country:

> Beside their sheltering cross of wall, the flock
> Feeds on in light, nor thinks of winter's shock . . .

2. See Wordsworth, *Representative Poems*, Arthur Beatty, ed. (Garden City, N.Y., Doubleday, Doran, 1937), pp. 33–5.

3. *Early Letters*, p. 35. Actually Wordsworth was disappointed by what little he did see of the Swiss peasant who, he thought, seemed to lack the true quality of benevolence characterizing the French peasant. *Ibid.* Many things would suggest that, except for the French peasant and Père Gerard in particular, it was only the peasantry of the Lake District who impressed him as a group. Dorothy writes of the peasants at Racedown, where they settled in 1795: "The peasants are miserably poor; their cottages are shapeless structures (I may almost say) of wood and clay—indeed they are not at all beyond what might be expected in savage life." *Idem*, p. 148. Wordsworth's impression of the peasantry around Nether Stowey may be inferred from the fact that he composed a picture of rural life showing its sordid side, calling it the "Somersetshire Tragedy." This was never published. See Harper, p. 269. The peasantry in Germany were not romantic in Dorothy's eyes: the women around Goslar she describes as regular beasts of burden, their stockings ungartered, their throats swollen, and each carrying a bottle of schnapps. *Early Letters*, p. 217. At Coleorton, where the Wordsworths made a long sojourn in 1806–7, they saw a peasantry who came to church poorly dressed and not too tidy. *Letters . . . Middle Years*, I, 77.

sketching out a series of satirical political poems; he was dashing off
Miltonic pamphlets to answer the writings of the absentee Bishop Watson who, as we have seen, was living placidly by the side of Windermere,
practicing horticulture. Wordsworth was the perfect young intellectual:
his dress was rather loud, I gather; a certain boldness and aggressiveness marked the whole person. When his political attention descended
from the realm of the universal, his eye was caught by the injustices
connected with war,[4] and also with the administration of poor relief.
He did not like the system of relief which prevented a man from receiving
any benefits while he still had any property left;[5] he did not like workhouse bastilles for the unemployed and unemployable.[6] But his social
attention had not yet been captured by the rural scene.

This shifting of his thought, which had clearly taken place by the
time the *Lyrical Ballads* appeared in their second edition of 1800, may
have several explanations. For one thing, his thought was becoming in
all ways less abstract. We note with great pleasure this tendency toward
definiteness in his dealing with nature itself. He forces himself to understand clearly the meaning of nature in human life. This influence, he
comes to understand, is resident in the fact that man is an imaginative
creature, motivated not by reason but by the image content of his mind.
This motivating imagery is inevitably in large part the imagery of nature
which eye and ear cannot choose but hear and see. Wordsworth's interpretation of nature in the language of the imagination many will feel
was the very essence of romanticism. It was the result of a determination
to be definite, to be real and concrete. His social thought too was simultaneously seeking the tangible, the concrete

> . . . the very world, which is the world
> Of all of us,—the place where, in the end,
> We find our happiness, or not at all.

It was inevitable that Wordsworth should find definite and particular
social subjects: and such a subject lay in the peasant. And at the same
time that this sense of real things was developing, his feelings were
clearly becoming more national in character. And nothing was more
central to the English tradition than the peasant-yeoman whom Wordsworth chose to celebrate. Other influences were moving him in this

4. The political evil of war is the principal theme of *Guilt and Sorrow* (1794).
5. See "The Last of the Flock."
6. See the "Old Cumberland Beggar." A late poem (1846) shows that some of these
sympathies had not died. It begins:
> I know an aged Man constrained to dwell
> In a large house of public charity . . .
The aged man of this poem, when living on alms in his cottage, had made the friendship
of a robin, who shared his bread. Now conveyed from his cottage to the poorhouse, he
feels so broken that he avoids all contact with other captives there. His injury is complete. Wordsworth, *Poetical Works*, pp. 530-1.

same direction, influences intellectual and personal. The cult of nature suggested the peasant, but Wordsworth's peculiar understanding of the peasant would make one hesitate to consider this influence primary. Finally, a strictly personal influence was surely active in the personality of Tom Poole, whom Wordsworth came to know well at Nether Stowey —a person who symbolized the yeoman in his mind.[7]

But these tendencies to consider the peasant would hardly have been precipitated had Wordsworth not been disturbed by the economic condition in which he found the peasantry of his native Lake country when he and Dorothy, coming home at last to the region that spoke their own accent, took up their residence at the Dove and Olive Branch cottage in those cold but wonderful days at the end of 1799. The Wordsworths settled themselves in perhaps the prettiest but least fashionable vale of the Lake country, the vale of Grasmere. The world of fashion had spread itself in the Ullswater and Windermere regions. The poet and especially his sister were pleasantly contemptuous of these smart areas, where the retainers were nattily got up in blue jackets and trousers, where party lights flickered at night from great houses.[8] The Wordsworths chose to associate with two classes of people, their few intellectual friends[9] and the natives. They were particularly close to the Fishers and the Ashburners who lived just across the road from Dove Cottage.[1] Dorothy's *Grasmere Journal* tells of their experiences in these first years back in the Lake country, from 1800 to 1803. There is much that is sad in the account. For one thing, it tells the story of Dorothy's loss of William through marriage, a sorrow which came to its climax for both of them in the great spring of 1802 which brought so many of the poems dealing with their childhood. But there is another sad story in the *Journal,* the story of Westmorland and Cumberland—a story of an ancient rural society falling into decay. I shall not attempt to give the whole picture of social misery and decay—the almost constant procession of beggars, some coming from their own native Cockermouth;[2]

7. Shortly after the appearance of "Michael," Wordsworth wrote to ask Poole his opinion of this poem, because in writing it, Wordsworth said, he often had the character of Poole before him. *Early Letters,* p. 266. He also wrote for Poole's opinion of the *Excursion. Letters . . . Middle Years,* II, 646.

8. See Dorothy's account of a day's excursion down to Windermere, with a maid of the Clarksons' as her companion. *Grasmere Journal,* June 8, 1802, in *Journals.*

9. Among these were Coleridge up at Keswick, the Reverend Mr. Sympson and his family up at Wythburn, the Clarksons over at Eusemere, and the Lloyds down a short way at Low Brathay, near Ambleside.

1. See Gordon Wordsworth's notes on these and other local families in *Journals,* I, 433–8, Appendix I.

2. "On the Rays we met a woman with two little girls, one in her arms, the other, about four years old, walking by her side, a pretty little thing, but half-starved. She had on a pair of slippers that had belonged to some gentleman's child, down at the heels, but it was not easy to keep them on, but, poor thing! young as she was, she walked carefully with them; alas, too young for such cares and such travels. The mother, when we accosted her, told us that her husband had left her, and gone off with another woman,

the scandalous drunkenness of the parson of pretty Grasmere church;[3] the wild philandering of the King of Patterdale who had impressed Gilpin as being such a worthy man when he saw him several years earlier on a journey through the Lakes.[4] I shall speak only of the hardship of the yeomen—or statesmen—the people who owned small estates. Such were the Fishers, who lived across from the Wordsworths: they were experiencing hard times; they had just recently recovered their "intake."[5] Molly Fisher, a sister, was glad to do housework for the Wordsworths, and John was glad to help with the gardening. One day John, overtaking Dorothy on her walk, said to her that "in a short time there would be only two ranks of people, the very rich and the very poor, 'for those who have small estates,' says he, 'are forced to sell, and all the land goes into one hand.' "[6] Mrs. Fisher told Dorothy one day about a certain Leonard Holmes who was so maddened by sickness and debts that he tried to give his wife back to his mother-in-law.[7] The Ashburners,

---

and how she 'pursued' them. Then her fury kindled, and her eyes rolled about. She changed again to tears. She was a Cockermouth woman, thirty years of age—a child at Cockermouth when I was. I was moved, and gave her a shilling—I believe 6d. more than I ought to have given." *Grasmere Journal*, May 4, 1802.

3. See the sentences at the end of Dorothy's moving account of a Lake country funeral, thought to be that of a pauper, Susan Shaelock: "The priest met us—he did not look as a man ought to do on such an occasion—I had seen him half-drunk the day before in a pot-house. Before we came with the corpse one of the company observed he wondered what sort of cue our Parson would be in! N.B. It was the day after the Fair." *Idem*, September 3, 1800.

4. Gilpin, traveling the Lake District in 1772, was inclined to see the peasantry through rose-colored Claude glasses. Their clothes, he notes, were made of an undyed russet brown wool, so that shepherd and sheep were dressed alike, "both in the simple livery of nature." Dieting on bread and milk, these peasants were the simple, innocent children of nature. At Patterdale Gilpin sought out one who was called the "King of Patterdale" because his house somewhat excelled the other cottages. He found the King fishing. ". . . If I were inclined," he writes, "to envy the situation of any potentate in Europe, it would be that of the king of Patterdale. The pride of Windsor and Versailles would shrink in a comparison with the magnificence of his dominions." Gilpin, *Observations*, II, 64.

From Dorothy Wordsworth now some years later we hear about the Queen of Patterdale. Peggy Ashburner, neighbor at Dove Cottage, brought this story over the hills, about the wife of Gilpin's fortunate peasant king: "She had been brought to drinking by her husband's unkindness and avarice. She was formerly a very nice tidy woman. She had taken to drinking but that was better than if she had taken to something worse (by this I suppose she meant killing herself). She said that her husband used to be out all night with other women and she used to *hear* him come in in the morning, for they never slept together—'Many a poor body, a wife like me, has had a working heart for her, as much stuff as she had.'" *Grasmere Journal*, December 22, 1801.

5. See Gordon Wordsworth's note, *Journals*, I, 434.

6. *Grasmere Journal*, May 18, 1800. Later in the *Guide through the District of the Lakes* Wordsworth wrote that the statesmen were selling their mortgaged lands to wealthy purchasers. Little cottages, "with all the wild graces that grew out of them," were disappearing to make way for new mansions: ". . . it is probable, that in a few years the country on the margin of the Lakes will fall almost entirely into the possession of gentry, either strangers or natives." *Prose Works*, II, 285-6.

7. *Grasmere Journal*, June 21, 1802.

other close neighbors, were a yeoman family living in reduced circumstances. Thomas Ashburner had taken to drawing coal from Keswick to supplement his income, and the Wordsworths were among his customers.[8] Another statesman's family, the Jacksons, were in severe financial difficulties because (so the gossip came to Dorothy) they had indulged too much in tea—with sugar![9] A little later than the period of the *Journal*, the Wordsworths were to interest themselves in behalf of the numerous orphans of George and Sarah Green, who were killed in an avalanche. George Green was not an untypical statesman: his little estate had been deeply mortgaged. He attempted to support his family with odd jobs and by selling peats in the summer. When the neighbors went to the house after the accident, they found a cupboard that was nearly bare—a couple of boilings of potatoes, a little meal, and a few pieces of dried mutton.[1]

The decline of these small proprietors—the statesmen—must have been underlined by the sight of the Lake country's becoming increasingly filled with tourists and summer residents. Rich Manchester merchants and Liverpool attorneys were putting up big summer homes that marred the entire side of a mountain.[2] The well-to-do were making the Lake country into a playground, and their manners were not a little disturbing. Hutchinson had reported that the duke of Portland kept a barge on Ullswater to entertain guests who came to see the mountains. This barge was armed with six cannon to be fired off during lunch on the lake so that the guests might hear their sevenfold echo through the mountains. Two French horns alternated with the cannon, sublimely and beautifully.[3] In the summer of 1806 the Wordsworths had living very near them a household who continually dressed in strange Eastern costumes: they wore green leather caps, turkey half boots, and long dressing gowns.[4] John Wilson, who should have been a sober resident, kept seven yachts on Windermere, and along with the indulged sons of Bishop Watson, sponsored local wrestling matches and cockfights.[5] The

---

8. See *idem*, May 17, 1800, and November 24, 1801.

9. *Idem*, June 21, 1802.

1. *Letters . . . Middle Years*, I, 182–3; see also, I, 178–9, 190–1.

2. *Early Letters*, p. 538. *Letters . . . Middle Years*, I, 19. See also *Inscriptions*, No. 7: "Written with a Slate Pencil upon a Stone, the Largest of a Heap Lying near a Deserted Quarry, upon One of the Islands at Rydal," Wordsworth, *Poetical Works*, p. 548.

3. William Hutchinson, *Excursion to the Lakes in Westmoreland and Cumberland, with a Tour through Part of the Northern Counties, in the Years 1773 and 1774* (London, 1776), pp. 62 ff. Portland also kept a barge at Keswick, complete with cannon. *Idem*, pp. 175 ff.

4. *Letters . . . Middle Years*, I, 51–2.

5. Elsie Swann, *Christopher North (John Wilson)* (Edinburgh, Oliver & Boyd, 1934), pp. 37–8. Gilpin reports that some gentlemen, who had come to live in the Lake District, had for want of racing put horses on rafts, which were floated to the center of the lake and there sunk. The gentlemen could wager on the horse to reach shore first. Gilpin, *Observations*, II, 67–9.

ways of the new residents of the Lake country must have made one specially conscious of the plight of the native rural population.

To understand the cause of the decline of the small proprietors of the Lake District, we must look somewhat closely at the economy of these mountain counties. It will be remembered that enclosure of open villages in the late eighteenth century belonged principally to the counties from York south to Dorset, particularly the Midlands. "The section of England affected by the Acts relating to open fields lay almost entirely between two lines, one drawn straight from Lyme Regis to Gloucester and from Gloucester to the Tees estuary, the second straight from Southampton to Lowestoft passing London a few miles to the west."[6] It is important to remember that the enclosure of open villages in this period occurred mainly in the south of England.

Now, in the country with which Wordsworth is associated, agriculture almost from the first had been conducted somewhat upon the pattern which enclosure was just effecting in the southern Midland counties —an agriculture of self-contained farms. In the *Guide through the District of the Lakes*[7] Wordsworth tells the story of the settlement of the Lake District. Prior to the time of the Reformation, the monks of Furness Abbey, interested in securing the northern border against Scottish raiders, encouraged settlement in these mountains and dales. Shepherds, creeping up into the valleys, gradually enclosed on the hillside their separate lands, marking with stone walls their fields of arable and pasture. But the shepherd-farming of Cumberland and Westmorland was at most only semienclosed. During the summer the dalesman pastured his sheep on the commons waste of the mountains. He was generally supposed to turn out only as many sheep as his enclosed lands would support during the winter months, such fields then being used through the summer for growing winter feed for the sheep. It often happened that a shepherd could add to his winter supply of food by buying forage, and thus he might have a larger number of sheep ranging the mountains in summer. The commons waste of these counties was rather overstocked, and, all late eighteenth-century surveyors observe, with a very poor grade of unimproved sheep that looked more like goats than sheep.[8]

The villages of these Lake counties, then, were, we may say, semienclosed, with walled-in arable and pasture but with very extensive commons waste on the mountains where all the sheep and cattle of a village grazed together. The kind of enclosure which affected the Midland southern counties, the enclosure of arable and pasture, did not apply to this region of partially self-contained farms. Another type of enclosure—the enclosure of the commons waste—did affect these great

6. Clapham, I, 19.   7. *Prose Works*, II, 256 ff.
8. John Bailey and George Culley, *General View of the Agriculture of the County of Cumberland* (London, 1794), p. 18.

open mountain wastes of the Lake District, though not seriously until the middle years of the nineteenth century.[9] But these statesmen of the dales were disappearing in 1800 when Wordsworth wrote the *Preface*. For causes of their decline one must look elsewhere than to enclosure.

The economic change affecting these small partly self-contained farms of the Lake country from about 1760 on, was, according to Wordsworth, the revolution in industry. The old economy of the Lake District was destroyed by the factory system which took away the textile industry. In the first years of the industrial revolution, he explains, factories, seeking water power, pushed up into this mountain country of streams, but the use of steam soon drew them back from these picturesque parts of the world to the regions of the coal mines. For this Wordsworth was grateful.[1] The landscape was saved, but not the people. The factory system ruined their domestic industry. Moreover, the energetic sons of these yeomen went to seek fortunes in the growing industrial sections of England. Wordsworth speaks of numerous Lake country freeholders as resident in London.[2]

Other causes have been advanced by others to explain the decline of the statesman. The reason Pringle gives in 1794 why "this class of men is daily decreasing" is the introduction of luxury.

The simplicity of ancient times is gone. Finer clothes, better dwellings, and more expensive viands are now sought after by all. This change of manners, combined with other circumstances which have taken place within the last forty years, has compelled many a *statesman* to sell his property, and reduced him to the necessity of working as a labourer in those fields which perhaps he and his ancestors had for many generations cultivated as their own.[3]

Clapham says the cause for the "constantly diminishing" number of statesmen in this period was "the misguided burdening of their land with portions for big families, which with fallen prices it could not carry."[4] But the usual explanation was Wordsworth's, and this we find accepted in Palgrave's *Dictionary of Political Economy:* "In Cumberland and Westmoreland the small 'statesmen' disappeared with the disappearance of the hand-loom."[5]

With *Lyrical Ballads* (1800) Wordsworth had clearly become a champion of domestic industry, the loss of which spelled ruin for the rural society of the Lake country. The pictures of different aspects of

9. See above, p. 21.

1. See *The Poetical Works of William Wordsworth*, W. Knight, ed. (Edinburgh, W. Paterson, 1882–89. 11 vols.), v, 11.

2. *Prose Works*, I, 235. See also Robert Southey, *Sir Thomas More: or Colloquies on the Progress and Prospects of Society* (2d ed. London, 1831. 2 vols.), II, 169.

3. Andrew Pringle, *General View of the Agriculture of the County of Westmoreland* (Edinburgh, 1794), pp. 40–1.

4. Clapham, I, 104.

5. See article, "Yeomen," and note authority given for this statement therein. *Dict. Pol. Econ.*

domestic industry in "Michael" and the "Brothers" are familiar to all. Lesser-known poems dealing with this ancient art came from Wordsworth's pen with a certain regularity through later years. In 1812 he wrote a "Song for the Spinning Wheel," based upon a Westmorland belief that at night while the sheep are asleep fairies help in the home with the spinning.

> Swiftly turn the murmuring wheel!
> Night has brought the welcome hour,
> When the weary fingers feel
> Help, as if from faery power;
> Dewy night o'ershades the ground;
> Turn the swift wheel round and round!
>
> Now, beneath the starry sky,
> Couch the widely-scattered sheep;—
> Ply the pleasant labour, ply!
> For the spindle, while they sleep,
> Runs with speed more smooth and fine,
> Gathering up a trustier line.
>
> Short-lived likings may be bred
> By a glance from fickle eyes;
> But true love is like the thread
> Which the kindly wool supplies,
> When the flocks are all at rest,
> Sleeping on the mountain's breast.[6]

In a sonnet written about 1819 Wordsworth describes one particular worth in vanishing domestic industry.

> Grief, thou hast lost an ever-ready friend
> Now that the cottage Spinning-wheel is mute;
> And Care—a comforter that best could suit
> Her froward mood, and softliest reprehend; . . .
> Even Joy could tell, Joy craving truce and rest
> From her own overflow, what power sedate
> On those revolving motions did await
> Assiduously—to soothe her aching breast;
> And, to a point of just relief, abate
> The mantling triumphs of a day too blest.[7]

These verses, incidentally, tell of Wordsworth's sensitivity to the normalizing effect of gentle motion, something which spinning wheels and poetry had in common. In a second sonnet, published in 1827 and addressed to S. H.,[8] Wordsworth speaks of the pleasure he feels in hearing

6. Wordsworth, *Poetical Works*, p. 163.
7. *Miscellaneous Sonnets*, Pt. I, No. 19, in Wordsworth, *Poetical Works*, p. 255.
8. *Miscellaneous Sonnets*, Pt. I, No. 20, in *ibid.*

her use the spinning wheel, not for fashion (for apparently ladies were then spinning for the effect!) but for a sincere love of the occupation. The poem ends with complaint against the factory system which had destroyed domestic industry.

> Venerable Art,
> Torn from the Poor! yet shall kind Heaven protect
> Its own; though Rulers, with undue respect,
> Trusting to crowded factory and mart
> And proud discoveries of the intellect,
> Heed not the pillage of man's ancient heart.

The counterpart of Wordsworth's praise of domestic industry is his indictment of the factory system, most fully voiced in Book Eighth of the *Excursion*. There you will remember the Wanderer describes the changing face of England—the expansion of agriculture so that all wastes are cultivated, the development of roads and canals, the astounding activity of England's harbors which were so greatly improved in the years of the Napoleonic wars. Finally he pictures the growth of towns out of hamlets and the pouring of country labor into the factories of these new cities. Repeating a great deal of the thought developed in the late eighteenth century when thinkers such as Adam Smith were more concerned for the welfare of those who produced luxuries than of those who consumed them, Wordsworth's Wanderer points out the danger of the factory system to morality, when children are made to associate with older workers and the father is working away from his home. He notes also the intellectual degeneration of the worker when, in the factory system of divided labor, the human being becomes simply a tool, an implement, a passive thing. The ill effects of factory labor are summed up in a picture of a young man emerging from a mill, his clothes covered with cotton or woolen flakes, his gait creeping, his eyes languid, his respiration quick and audible, his nervous system so dulled that he cannot feel the breeze or the heat of the sun.

In Wordsworth's writings the forces of evil which are destroying rural society are represented as industrial and bourgeois. This was a fair picture as far as Cumberland and Westmorland were concerned. But throughout England generally the landed class, who were improving and enclosing, were fully as responsible as the "cits" for the unfortunate condition of rural life. Wordsworth as a social poet would seem to have preferred to be faithful to the experience of his own northern counties rather than to the greater experience of England, which he certainly knew about.[9] Thus he was excused from attacking the landed class. In 1800 he was liking landlords better than in his revolutionary days; by 1818 he was so much for the big landed interests that he was pre-

9. See above, p. 38.

pared to make votes for the Lowther family by helping to set up twelve
new freeholders.[1]

The Shepherd's Dog

We must turn now to speak of Wordsworth's principal dealing with
the peasant. We have spoken perhaps rather too much at length about
domestic industry and the cottage. Poetry is not men's trades and tackle
and gear. Poetry is the science of feeling. The georgic element in Wordsworth's peasant poetry was only incidental. His first duty as a poet was
to interpret the emotional character of peasant life. It was here that he
found all that was precious. To understand Wordsworth's reading of
the peasant, we must look more largely at his performance as poet. There
are two varieties of feeling with which he, as a poet, was concerned.
He was first and principally interested in feeling as an imaginative
response to the imagery of nature. Such feeling I should call meta-
physical and philosophical. Second, he was concerned with those feelings
which are the affections—feelings that are homely and domestic. Now,
I think we are quite right in seeing a division in Wordsworth's poetry.
Feeling as imagination he reserved for himself and the child, our "best
philosopher"; feeling as affection he conferred, with just a slight air of
condescension and shame, upon the peasant world. Wordsworth would
seem to have entertained the assumption that there was something just
a little aristocratic about communing imaginatively with nature. The
whole school of rural reverie coming down to him from eighteenth-
century poetry would confirm the prejudice that this was something
almost too good for the common people. So these best things he kept
for himself, while giving to the peasant the life of the affections.[2]

1. Harper, p. 548.
2. One aspect of the affectionate life of the peasant which impressed Wordsworth was
the way the memory of the dead was kept alive in the minds of the living. In the
"Brothers" we see how the priest is able to give Leonard the complete account of his
brother, affection having prompted him to know all about this life and to preserve this
memory. No gravestones are to be found in this churchyard where they stand, nor are
such necessary: the priest's memory is stored with the records of this parish for 160 years
back (l. 188). The pastor in the *Excursion* carries in his affectionate memory a similar

But the gift was, nonetheless, a great one. Wordsworth made the peasant world in very large measure the world of emotion and passion, the world of tragic possibility. In thus interpreting humble and rustic life, Wordsworth was creating a new popular aesthetic which located the world of passionate feeling not in medieval castle or renaissance palace but rather in the cottage, on the soil of common life. The work of Hardy and Housman suggests the direct continuation of his aesthetic, the importance of which need not, however, be confined to literature that is rural in character. Wherever in literature the poetic character of common life has been recognized, we may claim something of a Wordsworthian influence.

The intensity of the affections among rural people Wordsworth made dependent partly upon the solitude of their lives. As Bradley has observed, solitude and soul are synonymous in Wordsworth. But the principal prop of the affections, Wordsworth thought, was a small property. A small farm is, as it were, a book on which a man's emotional life is written.[3] With its permanent objects—its trees, its stone walls, its brooks—associations have been made in the past with one's affectionate life—a love for a girl, or a love for one's child. Or with an object of the farm may be associated an act of kindness—the rescue of a sheep. Now, these objects feed the later years, recalling, even as the cuckoo brings back the visionary moments of childhood,[4] all past affections, making them grow from year to year in the groves of the heart.[5] Without such continuing associations, one's emotional life may become fickle, shallow, unstable. The peddler, as Wordsworth has unfortunately demon-

---

record of the lives of the dalesmen of Grasmere. These long and careful memories are perhaps the most impressive evidence Wordsworth offers of the strength of the affections of these people. The subtitle of "Solitude" for "Lucy Gray" is perhaps slightly ironical. Though Lucy lived far away on a lonely moor in solitude, local affections included her, and local imagination kept her alive, insisting that she still walked the moor, singing a solitary song. A dramatic instance of peasant affection is used by Wordsworth in the sonnet "Filial Piety," *Miscellaneous Sonnets,* Pt. III, No. 23, in Wordsworth, *Poetical Works,* p. 276. This is the story: Thomas Scarisbrick, living between Preston and Liverpool, was killed by a bolt of lightning while working on a turf stack in 1779. His son James completed the turf stack and in memory of his father kept it in continual repair through his lifetime. When he died in 1824, he left to his own children glasses and decanters engraved with the design of the turf stack standing between two trees.

3. See the letter to Charles James Fox of January 14, 1801 : "Their little tract of land serves as a kind of permanent rallying point for their domestic feelings, as a tablet upon which they are written which makes them objects of memory in a thousand instances when they would otherwise be forgotten." *Early Letters,* p. 262.

4. See *Excursion,* Bk. II, l. 347. See the "Cuckoo-Clock" (pub. 1842), which strangely enough preserves some of Wordsworth's finest feeling regarding this bird. Wordsworth, *Poetical Works,* p. 229.

5. See "Michael," ll. 65 ff. Wordsworth writes in the poem "To Cordelia M——":
Thing and thought
Mix strangely; trifles light, and partly vain,
Can prop, as you have learnt, our nobler being . . .
Wordsworth, *Poetical Works,* p. 480.

strated in Peter Bell, may be a thoroughly bad sort; and so may the city worker, moving from city to city and factory to factory, without permanent and, what is more important, beautiful objects of association around him. But in country life the affections must live, even in the degree that Michael feels affection for his son. Luke is present in every part of that small property: he lives particularly in the sheepfold which father and son had begun together. Thus I think we may see that Wordsworth, by making the affections dependent upon property, has fused, by a very natural use of the psychology of association, the sentimental and economic strands in his peasant poetry. Wordsworth was always at pains to tie the big knot of matter and spirit. This he accomplished in his nature poems by invoking the concept of the imagination. Here in his pastoral work he has used the psychology of association to a similar but, to be sure, a lesser end.

Coleridge, who was quite unsympathetic with the sentimental sociology of the Wordsworths, has said that Wordsworth's conception of peasant life was all a dream. Having himself a very slight sense of real things, Coleridge supposed that this reading of the peasant character was altogether the work of Wordsworth's own creative imagination. Coleridge was surely right in saying that the language of nature—that basic English—which Wordsworth would make the language of poetry, was not the speech of Lake country rustics. The slightest exposure to the dialect of Cumberland and Westmorland instructs one that this speech is about as close to a pure English as the dialect used by Burns.[6] If the emotional picture of the Lake region fashioned by Wordsworth was as untrue to life as the linguistic picture, it is less easy to decide. In any case it is, I think, quite clear that Wordsworth himself was increasingly unsatisfied by the peasantry of his own time. (Feelings were mutual, I may say: the belief prevailed at some Lake country hearths that Wordsworth was incapable of writing his own poems. Obviously they had been written for him by that amiable alcoholic, Hartley Coleridge![7]) Unsatisfied with the peasantry around him, Wordsworth came more and more to look for his golden people, not in the present but in the past. He became a local antiquarian, exploring the pastoral past in such prose writings as the essay On Epitaphs, the memoir of Robert Walker,[8] and the Guide through the District of the Lakes. The

6. See above, p. 21, n. 1.
7. See H. D. Rawnsley, "Reminiscences of Wordsworth among the Peasantry of Westmoreland," Wordsworthiana; a Selection from Papers Read to the Wordsworth Society, W. Knight, ed. (London, Macmillan, 1889), p. 96.
8. See Wordsworth, Poetical Works, pp. 910–15. This account of the Reverend Robert Walker, composed in 1819, was probably undertaken in preparation for writing the Guide to the district of the Lakes. Robert Walker, we are told, was born at Under-crag in Seathwaite in 1709, the youngest of twelve children. Since his eldest brother inherited the small family estate, Robert studied to be a scholar, partly in the local school, educating himself well enough to be ordained. About 1735 he became a curate and thereafter

rural poet became a haunter of country churchyards. The Grasmere churchyard, where he himself planted yews, became the center of his musings. Here the Pastor of the *Excursion* stands, making a sad embroidery of the lives of the worthy dead. A little later, in the Duddon sonnets, we are standing with Wordsworth in the graveyard at the Kirk of Ulpha, hearing him say that it is sweet

> . . . 'mid that wave-washed Churchyard to recline,
> From pastoral graves extracting thoughts divine . . .

In this late and very lovely volume, the antiquarian spirit has become a historical spirit, capable of feeling the length of time through all its geologic age.

While musing on the peasantry of the past, particularly of the eighteenth century which he loved better than did his critics, Wordsworth worked in the present to preserve and recreate a democratic agrarian society. In 1801 he sent to Fox a copy of the second edition of *Lyrical Ballads,* along with a letter urging this statesman to concern himself with the peasant proprietor threatened by the factory system. Fox seems to have missed the point entirely, replying that he was very much moved by such poems as "The Mad Mother," "The Idiot Boy," etc! Never a communist like the early Coleridges and Southeys, never rising for any sustained period to the Franciscan feelings expressed in "Resolution and Independence," Wordsworth, while he came to approve

---

served his parish 66 years with devotion, always refusing better livings. He was a hospitable clergyman, providing broth at his table for the families who came a long distance to church. He taught school in the church, with the communion table for desk, five and one-half eight-hour days a week. He also acted as scrivener for the community. In spite of his constant industry he preserved, says Wordsworth, the finer parts of character and mind. He read and studied his Bible, using Burkitt's commentaries for the New Testament. Understanding and loving tradition, he was devoted to the Establishment, and boasted that there was no dissenter in his cure. Moreover, he was "a passionate admirer" of nature. He gathered flies and insects, knew plants and fossils, and was a constant observer of the atmosphere. The night before his death, in his ninety-third year, he was assisted outdoors to look at the sky. "How clear the moon shines to-night!" he observed.

Wordsworth makes it evident in the memoir that he understood how important domestic industry was in the livelihood of this Lake country clergyman. While hearing the children recite their lessons, he spun on a small wheel, "like Shenstone's schoolmistress," says Wordsworth. Evenings at home he used a large wheel, walking betimes. The spinnings of his household, in weights of 16 or 32 pounds, he carried on his back to market 7 or 8 miles away, sometimes in the dead of winter. The family pew in church was lined with woolen cloth of his own spinning. He and his wife, both dying in the year 1802, left behind "a large store of webs of woollen and linen cloth." Wordsworth writes: "Upon the Seathwaite Brook, at a small distance from the parsonage, has been erected a mill for spinning yarn; it is a mean and disagreeable object, though not unimportant to the spectator, as calling to mind the momentous changes wrought by such inventions in the frame of society—changes which have proved especially unfavourable to these mountain solitudes. So much had been effected by those new powers, before the subject of the preceding biographical sketch closed his life, that their operation could not escape his notice, and doubtless excited touching reflections upon the comparatively insignificant results of his own manual industry." Wordsworth, *Poetical Works,* p. 914.

great landed estates as a rallying ground for national affections,[9] was nonetheless a lifelong defender of small properties.[1] He opposed the Reform Bill of 1832 because it allowed the vote to people without property in the land—that property which he thought central to the emotional and moral life of a man. If this position seems reactionary, let us not forget that Wordsworth would have been glad to increase the number of voters by reinstating into their properties the thousands of yeomen whose holdings had gone into the hands of great farmers and rich manufacturers. In 1844 Wordsworth finally put up a crotchety opposition to the Kendal-Windermere railway because it would cut up so many sacred small properties.

Coleridge has said that the ideals behind the French Revolution were physiocratic; and the late Professor Beatty has remarked that Wordsworth was greatly influenced by these French agrarians and by the poets who spoke their doctrines.[2] Both these comments are misleading, if not exactly untrue. Physiocratic agrarianism was not democratic and it was

9. *Prose Works,* I, 222–3.

1. In the *Excursion* of 1814 there may be some backsliding, for here he does not seem to have insisted upon property as the basis of the affections. The affections seem rather to rest in religion, in an allegiance to the teachings of Christ whose life is light and truth to the "baptized imaginations" of these dalesmen. There is, I believe, only one obvious mention of small properties in the *Excursion,* and that in connection with the Wanderer himself, who was born on a small hereditary farm.

But that fine poem, the "Pass of Kirkstone," written in 1817, sounds the note of property again. See the lines beginning,
> Ye ploughshares sparkling on the slopes!
> Ye snow-white lambs that trip
> Imprisoned 'mid the formal props
> Of restless ownership!

Wordsworth, *Poetical Works,* p. 214.

2. Let me quote from the general introduction of Beatty's edition of Wordsworth's *Representative Poems:* ". . . he shows an acquaintance with those eighteenth-century French poets, who, years before 1789, championed the cause of the poor and of agriculture, the foundation of any stable society. These are for the most part only names now, but Jacques Delille is famous for his translation of the *Georgics* of Virgil, which is propaganda for the simple life and for agriculture. Its long preliminary discourse in prose contains all that Wordsworth says in 1800 about natural language and the simple life: this Wordsworth very obviously appropriates. Delille carried on his agricultural theme in the poem *The Gardens;* and the poems of Rosset, Roucher, and Saint Lambert combine to present agriculture, freedom, anti-slavery, to protest against taxes on grain, the grants of special favours to the rich, and all the shocking inequalities of the time. With these poets Wordsworth was familiar, and their pages became more vivid when he found that men in real life were actually suffering from these impediments to happiness. The doctrines of Saint Lambert sprang into sudden life when Wordsworth read the physiocratic theories of agriculture as expounded by the statesman, Turgot, and saw the system of oppression which rendered the statesman's vision impossible of realization." P. xxxvi.

Again, from his introduction to *An Evening Walk:* "Wordsworth was deeply indebted to the work of the French poets Delille, Rosset, and Roucher, who first introduced him to the problems involved in the real representation of rural life and the use of the real language of men. And there can be no doubt that he was acquainted with the work of Jean François Saint-Lambert (1716–1803), whose poem *Les Saisons,* 1769, expresses the attitude of the physiocrats in glorifying the importance of agriculture and the agriculturist to the nation." P. 11.

hardly revolutionary. Wordsworth's agrarian thought could not easily be founded in such economic theory. If one would look for an economist with an outlook similar to Wordsworth's, surely it would be ~~Adam Smith~~, whose liberalism and individualism Wordsworth's social poetry would seem in large measure to enforce.[3] But there is one small deficiency in Wordsworth's agrarian liberalism which does call for a moment's comment. Wordsworth held up Cumberland and Westmorland as ideals. These two counties had been indeed remarkable for their large number of small properties, owned by the "statesmen." But ownership in England has not always meant what it means in America. Ownership was not without its restrictions, and in Cumberland and Westmorland these restrictions had been greater than in other perhaps more enlightened parts of England. A majority of the statesmen, or yeomen, of these counties were not freeholders, whose old feudal services had been commuted into a small quit rent, as the only remaining limitation upon ownership. They were rather, for the greater part, copyholders, not freeholders, and accordingly their properties were subject to fines when the lord or the tenant died—"eventful fines"; furthermore, services, or boon days, were required of such tenants.[4] The Lake District was not quite the land of "perfect equality" which Wordsworth calls it.[5] The darkness of feudalism lingered over it—a darkness that seemed greater, the further north one went in the British Isles. Several late eighteenth-century observers complained of these feudal survivals in the landholding of Wordsworth's counties.[6] But no complaint came from Wordsworth himself. He was silently satisfied, it would seem, that a touch of feudalism should remain in society, that independence should not be complete and entire.

3. In his book on *The Statesmanship of Wordsworth* (Oxford, Clarendon Press, 1917), A. V. Dicey has shown how influential the poetry of Wordsworth was in finding the liberal ideals of nationalism at the critical time when England needed "a cause" on which to fight the Napoleonic empire. Wordsworth helped England find the cause of a Europe of free and independent nations, a cause that still has meaning today. His contribution to national liberalism is clearly seen, but his contribution to the ideal of individual independence has not been quite so definitely recognized.

4. Bailey and Culley write in their *General View of the Agriculture of the County of Cumberland*, p. 11: "There are probably few counties, where *property in land* is divided into such small parcels as in Cumberland; and those small properties so universally occupied by the owners; by far the greatest part of which are held under the lords of the manors, by that species of vassalage, called *customary tenure*; subject to the payment of fines and heriots, on alienation, death of the lord, or death of tenant, and the payment of certain annual rents, and performance of various services, called *Boon-days*, such as getting and leading the lord's peats, plowing and harrowing his land, reaping his corn, haymaking, carrying letters, &c. &c. whenever summoned by the lord.

"We cannot pretend to be accurate, but believe, that *two thirds* of the county are held by this kind of tenure, in tenements from 5£. to 50£. a-year; but the generality are from 15£. to 30£."

Estimates of the amount of freehold and customary tenure in Cumberland are to be found in the Housman footnotes throughout William Hutchinson's *History of the County of Cumberland* (Carlisle, 1794. 2 vols.).

5. *Prose Works*, II, 263.

6. Bailey and Culley regarded the amount of customary tenure in this county as a principal impediment to better agricultural methods. "One great obstacle to improve-

I have said that Wordsworth remained faithful throughout his life to the ideal of an agrarian society of small proprietors. This I believe to be true. At the same time one must recognize the fact that the later Wordsworth espoused thoughts and sentiments quite at variance with old opinions he continued to hold. This indeed was the pattern of his later thought: he was not altogether reactionary; rather it would seem that he tried a little to turn the corner into the Victorian age, at the same time keeping old beliefs—beliefs which must have been necessary for the security of the personality, if for no other reason. So we see in the later Wordsworth agrarian feeling expressed along with sentiments quite contradictory. In 1832 he could oppose the Reform Bill as giving a grace to an industrial, propertyless society. The next year he could be much more in tune with his age. In 1833 Wordsworth is traveling in Scotland. He had been there two years before and at that time had been feeling particularly cheerless about old Scotland. This year, however, finds him in different spirits, and he is pleased by what he sees prophetic of the new age. A factory town like Greenock appears prosperous, happy, clean.

> Where be the wretched ones, the sights for pity?
> These crowded streets resound no plaintive ditty:—

---

ment, seems to arise, from a laudable anxiety in the customary tenants, to have their little patrimony descend to their children. These small properties (loaded with fines, heriots and boon days, joined to the necessary expence [sic] of bringing up and educating a numerous family) can only be handed down, from father to son, by the utmost thrift, hard labour, and penurious living; and every little saving being hoarded up for the payment of the *eventful fine*, leaves nothing for the expences of travelling, to see improved modes of culture; and to gain a knowledge of the management and profits of different breeds of stock; and be convinced, by ocular proofs, that their own situations are capable of producing similar advantages. And even should they be half inclined to adopt a new practice, prudence whispers, that, should the experiment fail, it would require the savings of many years to make good the deficiency." *General View of the Agriculture of the County of Cumberland,* pp. 44-5.

At the conclusion of his *Excursion to the Lakes* (1776 ed.), pp. 292-4, Hutchinson puts in the following complaint against the kind of land tenure existing in these Lake counties, a complaint he is to repeat in his *History of the County of Cumberland.* "I cannot take my leave of the counties of Westmorland and Cumberland, without observing on the nature of the tenures of their lands.—The most perfect relics of the old feudal tenures are to be found there, of any part in this kingdom:—many of the manors are customary, and the tenants hold by copy of their Lord's court roll;—some of them under a certain fine, payable on the demise of lord or tenant, or alienation by the tenant, together with an annual rent or payment to the lord;—others are so base as to be subject to an arbitrary fine, to be set by the lord on the like changes; so that if he has any dislike to his copyholder, he can impose on him the full value of his estate before he admits him on his roll.—These tenements, in their nature, are not devisable by will, nor are they assets subject to debts in the hands of the heir;—if a mortgage deed is not renewed within the term of three years, the mortgagee is admitted tenant by alienation, and on paying his fine, his enrollment operates as a foreclosure; the wives are dowable in a full moiety, and in some manors the eldest female heir, in default of males, inherits. Such extensive common rights appertain to the lands, that in many parts a man of six pounds a year brings up a family on his income.

"Many other badges of servility attend these tenures, and are exercised to this day; others are changed into money payments."

As from the hive where bees in summer dwell,
Sorrow seems here excluded . . .[7]

The Cuckoo

He travels through the Western Isles by steamboat, whose straight, regular course he finds depressing. He does not altogether enjoy looking at scenery from the crowded deck of this "dull monster," surrounded by a sooty crew.[8] Indeed, modern traveling is so disturbing that after landing at Staffa he must linger alone at the cave of Fingal to reverence the sight undistracted.[9] Yet, despite personal inconvenience and annoyance, he will hail the steamboat and other new developments in transportation, the viaduct and the railway.

> Motions and Means, on land and sea at war
> With old poetic feeling, not for this,
> Shall ye, by Poets even, be judged amiss!
> Nor shall your presence, howsoe'er it mar
> The loveliness of Nature, prove a bar
> To the Mind's gaining that prophetic sense
> Of future change, that point of vision, whence
> May be discovered what in soul ye are.
> In spite of all that beauty may disown
> In your harsh features, Nature doth embrace
> Her lawful offspring in Man's art; and Time,
> Pleased with your triumphs o'er his brother Space,
> Accepts from your bold hands the proffered crown
> Of hope, and smiles on you with cheer sublime.[1]

Wordsworth's later poetry does not leave us without the Victorian vision of factory chimneys pouring their black smoke over Gothic churches.

7. Wordsworth, *Poetical Works,* p. 475.
8. "On the Frith of Clyde," *idem,* p. 471.
9. "Cave of Staffa" (1) (2), *idem,* p. 473.
1. "Steamboats, Viaducts, and Railways," *idem,* p. 477.

Index

Adam, Margaret I., 27
Agricultural improvement, agricultural societies, 5–6, 29, 32, 63; breeding, 2, 8, 9, 13; canals, 43–4; clergy as improvers, 4, 6–7, 19; cult of the gentleman farmer, 10–12, 48; decade of 1760–70, 2–3; and depopulation, 43; and enclosure, 12–26, 39–40; English eminence in agriculture, 2, 5, 7, 32, 69, 74; the improvers, 3–5, 16; and optimism, 8; and population, 17–19, 83; professorships of agriculture, 3, 29; prosperity, 58–61; sheepshearings, 4, 5, 62–3; Tullian farming, 1–2, 4, 26, 29, 70; turnip, 2, 4, 10, 19
Aikin, Anna Laetitia, 44
Alison, Archibald, 24–5
America, 27, 43, 71, 83
Amery, G. D., 3
Anderson, Robert, 49, 54–5
Annals of Agriculture, x, 3, 4, 5, 6, 7, 11, 17, 18, 22, 23, 59, 60, 61, 62, 83, 84
Ashburner, Mr. and Mrs. Thomas, 89, 90–1
Ashton, Thomas S., vii

Bailey, John, 21, 92, 101–2
Bakewell, Robert, 2, 4, 7, 59
Ballad, 36, 41, 45, 46, 50–2, 54–5, 60
Balsamo, Paolo, 18
Baudeau, Abbé Nicolas, 70–2, 75
Beatty, Arthur, 87, 100
Beer, Max, 84
Beggar, the, 61–2, 88, 89
Bell, Howard J., 32
Bentham, Jeremy, 20
Berkeley, Bishop George, 31
Bewick, Thomas, vii–viii, xi, 9, 23, 39–42, 44, 55–6, 59; woodcuts, 9, 12, 19, 26, 39, 47, 55, 58, 64, 74, 86, 96, 103
Blake, William, vii, 26, 36–8, 57–8
Blamire, Susanna, 55
Bloomfield, Robert, 59
Blunden, Edmund, 44
Board of Agriculture, 3, 5, 11, 14, 16, 21, 23, 27, 62
Boo, Prince Lee, 7
Bradley, Andrew C., 97
British Georgics, 9
Bronowski, Jacob, vii
Burke, Edmund, vii, 24
Burns, Robert, 26, 28–9, 48–9, 50, 51, 53–4, 56, 98
Butts, W., 84

Canals, 43–4, 95
Cannan, Edwin, xi, 31
Carlyle, Alexander J., and Mrs. R. Monti Carlyle, 34
Carlyle, Thomas, 36, 64
Cartwright, Edmund, 4
Cestre, Charles, 44
Chapman, Robert W., 27
Child labor, 37, 80, 95
China, 66, 75, 79
Chinard, Gilbert, 83
Cincinnatus, 48, 83
City, the, 13, 18, 35, 39, 71–2, 81–2, 84–5
Clapham, John H., x, 14, 15–16, 21–2, 92, 93
Clare, John, 26, 44–7, 60
Classical agrarian feeling, 11–12, 47–8
Clutton-Brock, Arthur, 18
Cobbett, William, xi, 1, 17, 63
Coke, Thomas William, of Holkham, 3–4, 17, 62–3
Cole, George D. H., 15
Coleridge, Hartley, 98
Coleridge, Samuel Taylor, 22, 38, 42, 44, 67, 89, 98, 99, 100
Commons, defined, 12; enclosure of, 19–26, 40–1, 45–7; the laborer and, 20; parliamentary acts affecting, 21
Cone, Carl B., vii
Cottages, picturesque, 24–6
"The Cotter's Saturday Night," 26, 28–9
Cowley, Abraham, 7, 11
Cowper, William, 34–6, 47
Crabbe, George, 26, 32–4
Crane, Ronald S., 30, 31, 32
Cromwell, Oliver, 7, 25
Cross, Wilbur L., 19
Culley, George, 21, 92, 101–2
Currie, James, 29, 49
Curtis, Lewis P., 19
Curtler, William H. R., x, 5, 6, 26, 60, 62

Davies, Rev. David, 22, 43
Dawe, George, 56
Day, Thomas, 42, 47–8, 51, 57
De Selincourt, Ernest, x, xi, xii, 53
Deserted Village, The, 30–2, 41, 43, 54, 57
Dicey, Albert V., 101
Division of labor, 18, 95; Adam Smith on, 80–1
Dodsley, A., 83
Dodsley, Robert, 1–2
Dupont de Nemours, Pierre S., 66, 68, 83